SCHOOL SHOOTINGS

Other books in the At Issue series:

SCHOOL SHOOTINGS

Laura K. Egendorf, *Book Editor*

Daniel Leone, *President*
Bonnie Szumski, *Publisher*
Scott Barbour, *Managing Editor*

An Opposing Viewpoints® Series

Greenhaven Press, Inc.
San Diego, California

Library of Congress Cataloging-in-Publication Data

School shootings / Laura K. Egendorf, book editor.
        p. cm. — (At issue)
     Includes bibliographical references and index.
     ISBN 0-7377-1276-7 (lib. bdg. : alk. paper) —
ISBN 0-7377-1275-9 (pbk. : alk. paper)
     1. School violence. 2. School shootings. I. Egendorf, Laura K.,
1973– II. At issue (San Diego, Calif.)

LB3013.3 .S36   2002
371.7'82—dc21   2001042896
                                                                              CIP

© 2002 by Greenhaven Press, Inc.
10911 Technology Place, San Diego, CA 92127

Printed in the U.S.A.

Every effort has been made to trace owners of copyrighted material.

Table of Contents

WITHDRAWN

Introduction

Since 1995, more than thirty students and teachers have been killed and approximately one hundred have been wounded as a result of shootings at American schools. Towns throughout the nation, from California to Pennsylvania, have been affected by school violence. The deadliest of these school shootings occurred on April 20, 1999, at Columbine High School in Littleton, Colorado. Dylan Klebold and Eric Harris killed twelve students and a teacher and wounded twenty-three others before turning the guns on themselves. However, despite the seemingly high number of casualties at Columbine and other campuses, many people disagree as to whether school shootings are a widespread problem or rare incidents that attract undue attention because of their dramatic and horrifying nature.

The Centers for Disease Control and Prevention's Youth Risk Behavior Survey, which is taken every other year, provides statistics on the threat of school violence. According to the 1995 survey: "More than 7% [of high school students] had carried a gun. More than 8% of the students surveyed reported being threatened or injured with a weapon on school property during the previous 12 months." For the study's most recent year, 1999, the percentages had fallen to 4.9 percent and 7.7 percent, respectively. Even though the numbers have fallen, the problem of students bringing weapons to school has not been wholly eliminated.

Another indication of the problem of school shootings is that students are increasingly worried about coming to school due to fear of being a victim of a shooting. The percentage of students who had missed at least one day of school during the previous thirty days because they felt unsafe on campus or traveling to and from school increased between 1997 and 1999, from 4 percent to 5.2 percent. In addition, polls show that parents are increasingly concerned about the dangers facing their children. In a September 1999 Gallup poll, 47 percent of parents surveyed said they feared for their children's safety at school. Perhaps because several of the shootings have occurred in smaller Southern towns, 54 percent of rural parents and 56 percent of Southern parents expressed these concerns. Another poll, this one conducted by the *Wall Street Journal*, echoes those findings. Seventy-one percent of its respondents believed that a shooting was likely to take place at their children's school.

Although these polls suggest widespread fear over the likelihood of a nearby school shooting, some commentators contend that the problem is exaggerated and that too much attention has been placed on school shootings at the expense of the actual facts about violence. Lori Dorfman, director of the Berkeley Media Studies Group, and Vincent Schiraldi, director of the Justice Policy Institute, argue that school shootings are particularly rare occurrences. They write: "School-associated violent deaths have dropped 72% since 1992, and there was a less than one-in-3-million chance that a youth would be killed in a school [in 2000]." However, they note, the public is misled by inaccurate media coverage, writing: "68% of local TV news stories about violence in California involved youth, while youth made up only 14% of violent crime arrests in the state." Mike Males, who has also researched media coverage of youth violence, supports the conclusions of Dorfman and Schiraldi. He contends that, despite the various school shootings, today's youth are considerably less violent than their counterparts in the 1970s: "The latest (1999) [California] crime figures report murder by white youths at a record low, 65% below its 1970s rate." He also writes that of the 150,000 gun-related homicides that occurred in the 1990s, only 150 occurred at or around a school.

In addition to the debate over the frequency of school shootings, disputes exist on how to best end such assaults. Two types of solutions have been suggested for ending school shootings. The first approach focuses on preventing shootings by increasing security. Examples of this approach include placing metal detectors at the entrances to schools, hiring security guards or off-duty police officers to patrol the campuses, removing lockers so students cannot hide weapons, and instituting zero-tolerance policies that expel or suspend students who are found in possession of a weapon. These safeguards are commonplace in many school districts. For example, every high school in the Los Angeles Unified School District is given hand-held metal detectors and staffed with district police officers. In school districts throughout Washington State, officials have installed emergency phone systems and established tip lines on which students can call and report threats. Columbine High responded to the shootings by adding surveillance cameras and security officers (it had an on-campus armed law enforcement officer on campus when the massacre occurred), although it has not installed metal detectors.

Some commentators maintain that increasing security is the wrong solution because it does not address the problems facing adolescents, such as feelings of alienation or fears of being bullied. In several of the school shootings, the perpetrators have been described as outsiders who were frequently teased or bullied, which has led to speculation that bullying can have violent consequences.

People who oppose increased security suggest that another solution to school shootings is to teach students how to better understand each other and provide them with outlets to discuss their problems. In his book *Nobody Left to Hate: Teaching Compassion After Columbine*, Stanford University psychologist Elliot Aronson suggests that high schools are largely hostile environments and that schools should take steps to ensure that students become more accepting of each other. He contends that cooperative teaching methods can help reduce the tensions that can lead troubled adolescents to take revenge against their classmates. In cooperative learning, students are divided into groups to study a topic. Each student in the group researches an aspect of the topic and shares what he or she has learned. Because the group will be tested on all components of the project, it is disadvantageous for students to ignore or ridicule any of their coworkers. Another way in which schools have helped students cope with the pressures of adolescence is on-campus health clinics that provide mental health services. According to James Sterngold of the *New York Times*, the number of such clinics has increased from 200 to 1,380 since 1991.

Although debate exists over the prevalence of school shootings as compared to other types of violence, each shooting is undoubtedly a tragedy for its campus and the surrounding community. These acts leave communities searching for answers as to why they happen and how they can be prevented in the future. In *School Shootings: At Issue*, the authors examine why the attacks at Columbine and other campuses have occurred and what solutions might help end the problem.

1

Bullying Can Lead to School Shootings

Nick Gillespie

Nick Gillespie, the editor-in-chief of Reason *magazine, is a writer whose articles and editorials have appeared in publications such as the* New York Times, Washington Post, *and* National Review.

Many students are harassed by their peers at school. Although this bullying does not excuse the school shootings occurring across America, it does produce some empathy for students like Dylan Klebold and Eric Harris, the teenagers behind the fatal shootings at Columbine High School in Colorado. Schools need to be aware of the conformist and repressive atmosphere they create with their emphasis on order. School officials must take steps to ensure that adolescence is not a painful experience for its students.

The victims of the Columbine High School shootings in Littleton, Colorado, have been buried, if not fully laid to rest. Even as the incident fades from sharp memory and the schools empty for summer vacation, there's a good reason why this terrifying incident should haunt our national consciousness longer than similar tragedies in Springfield, Oregon; Jonesboro, Arkansas; West Paducah, Kentucky; and Pearl, Mississippi. It's not simply because the death toll is so much higher than in past massacres, or the mayhem so much more calculated.

Understanding Klebold and Harris

However horrific, the actions of other schoolyard gunmen such as Kip Kinkel or Luke Woodham can be readily understood as stemming from individual pathologies and, hence, not particularly reflective of broader social issues. In contrast, the Columbine shootings can be seen as implicating not only the killers' own sick, twisted minds, but a school culture which humiliated and tormented them in ways that are all too familiar to most Americans.

The result has been a highly uncomfortable—but strangely understandable—empathy for Dylan Klebold and Eric Harris. When *Newsweek* quotes a classmate saying that the two walked the halls of Columbine "with their heads down, because if they looked up they'd get thrown into lockers and get called a 'fag,'" who doesn't exactly understand the anger and frustration such abuse inspires? When *Time* reports that they were routinely physically threatened and taunted as "dirt bags" and "inbreeds," who doesn't feel a twinge of outrage on their behalf? In a strange way—and one starkly at odds with the early media narrative of Klebold and Harris as isolated, inhuman killing machines—the pair almost emerged from the coverage as high school everymen, stand-ins for every bad memory of adolescent injury in a school setting.

We cannot even imagine schools that are not just a few steps removed from Lord of the Flies.

After writing a column on the shooting for the World Wide Web site Slashdot.org, journalist Jon Katz was surprised to receive a deluge of "jarring testimonials from kids, adults, men and women" that while in no way exonerating the killers, "explained more—a lot more—about Littleton than all the vapid media stories about video violence, Goths, [and] game-crazed geeks." As one respondent put it, "I'm a geek under the skin . . . was a state champ in the high jump, and the leading scorer on the track team, so I was not quite the outcast that some . . . geeks are, but I understand what they are going through." Or, as another wrote, "I was much like those kids when I was in school—weird, cast out, not much liked, alienated, all that sort of thing. . . . I used to imagine bringing weaponry to school and making the fuckers who made my life miserable beg for mercy."

Such responses are hardly limited to the sorts of technophilic "geeks" likely to surf the Web. Virtually everyone I spoke with after the shootings—people ranging from college professors to package-delivery men, from lawyers to current high school students, from ex-jocks to ex-band members—expressed some understanding of and appreciation for what they took to be the killers' mind-set. These ranged from the comments of a gay friend who half-jokingly wished he'd had access to guns while in high school to the confession of an athletic standout who felt sick at the bullying company he kept during the same years.

How schools affect adolescence

Needless to say, nothing shifts the final responsibility for violence away from its perpetrators. But such unexpected fellow-feeling should give us great pause, even as it also helps to explain the recurring motif of school-related alienation and discomfort in popular works as varied in age, tone, setting, and genre as *The Catcher in the Rye, Rebel Without a Cause, Blackboard Jungle, The Outsiders, The Basketball Diaries, Carrie,* Pink Floyd's *The Wall, Heathers,* MTV's *Daria, Buffy the Vampire Slayer,* and *She's All That.* These and similar works are not all violent, but all in some way address the stultifying effects of a school culture that is widely acknowledged as nasty and brutish, conformist and repressive—and, all too often, brazenly anti-intellectual. It is almost as if we cannot even imagine schools that are not just a few steps removed from *Lord of the Flies*.

Of course, adolescence is at best a difficult, awkward period. It's a time when children move toward adulthood in tentative, often faltering steps—a process of individuation and identity creation that necessarily implies discomfort, discontent, and bouts of real and imagined alienation and ostracism. The question is whether schools tend to exacerbate those feelings or to sublimate them to some higher end. Do they reduce the pain of adolescence or add to it? The general understanding of Klebold's and Harris' experiences strongly suggests the former.

In a strange coincidence, a previously planned special issue of *Rolling Stone* on "the new teen spirit" hit the newsstands shortly after the Columbine shootings. Part of the magazine, tellingly titled "When Everything Sucked," was devoted to reminiscences by musicians and actors about their teen years. One major theme was how harrowing high school was, psychically as well as physically. "It was brutal—like a prison," said rock star Rob Zombie, in a typical comment. To be sure, the dreadlocked Zombie—like the other participants in the article—is hardly a representative sample. But he is onto something nonetheless: American high schools often do resemble prisons, and not simply because they tend to be large, impersonal institutions filled with gangs, drugs, and cops or because they tend to prize order above all else. They are filled with many people who would rather be elsewhere.

It is, of course, wrong to hope for anything decent to come out of a tragedy like the one at Columbine High. But perhaps some small scrap of good can be salvaged if it forces us to envision—and to create—schools that do not become personal hells for so many kids.

2

Bullying Is Not a Valid Reason for School Shootings

Dorothy Rabinowitz

Dorothy Rabinowitz is an author, Pulitzer Prize–winning commentator, and member of the Wall Street Journal's *editorial board.*

Some students experience bullying from their peers at school. However, bullying should not be used as an excuse for school shootings. By placing so much emphasis on the dangers of harassment, modern society has turned the shooters into the victims. Charles Andrew Williams, the shooter at Santee High School in southern California, and other assailants disregard society's taboos against murder in order to commit these crimes.

By now, thanks to the new school massacre, there can hardly be an American who hasn't heard of the latest newly discovered menace to the nation's peace and security—namely, bullying. Yes, there are people here and there who will wonder what exactly is new about school bullies and teens who suffer from teasing, but they are, of course, people who fail to appreciate our media's need to find answers to seemingly unfathomable mysteries. Answers, say, that could explain what it is that causes students to take guns to school and shoot their classmates.

It was doubtless with great relief that they discovered an initial answer after the massacres at Columbine High School in Littleton, Colorado, where, it was rumored, the two shooters had been outcasts of sorts, objects of bullying. For endless days following the Columbine rampage, we heard about their alienation, and about the need to listen to the anger of the young.

Sympathy for the killer

No one who remembers the goings-on about the anger of the two killers—a subject that elicited mind-numbing hours of reverential oratory—can be much surprised at the current discourse about [March 2001's] attacks at Santana High School in Santee, California, or the speed with which that event became transformed into another object lesson about alienation, youthful anger, and the dangers posed by school bullies.

As was true after Littleton, network bookers spent blood, sweat and tears looking for guests who could talk about those involved—but it was left to [the] "Today" show to come up with what must have seemed a bonanza. Here was a former girlfriend of 15-year-old Charles Andrew Williams, the perpetrator, and her mother. In the course of this interview, we learned of Andy's goodness, and his sensitivity, how everybody back home in his old Maryland neighborhood adored him and still loved him and wanted him to come home. They did not, the mother of the girl allowed, between paeans to Andy's goodness, "agree with what he did."

The explanation for the behavior of the shooters has a lot more to do with the premises of the world they inhabit than with bullying.

Agree with what he did? We are speaking of murder here, of two young men dead. Still, there was something about this language, its otherworldly detachment, that did not seem out of place in an interview which consisted entirely of testimonials to Andy's troubles, his loneliness, all of it interspersed with expressions of understanding from Katie Couric about how hard all this must be for them.

At no point in the interview did it occur to the normally inquisitive Ms. Couric to ask if there wasn't something a bit unbalanced, say, in this singularly glowing testimony to Andy, who had just cold-bloodedly mowed down everybody he laid eyes on. All that notwithstanding, one could have learned a lot about the reasons for the behavior of the Andys of this world, from these guests.

Overemphasizing bullying

The explanation for the behavior of the shooters has a lot more to do with the premises of the world they inhabit than with bullying. It is a world that has elevated pains like harassment—bullying—to a crime second only to homicide. And it is a world whose premises the young, like Andy Williams, have entirely internalized. Given the assumptions of a society that stresses, as ours now does, the inviolable right to freedom from insult, and from all the slings and arrows that are and always will be a part of life's experience, it shouldn't be surprising that a teenager who perceives himself as bullied will absorb the message that he has been made victim of a monstrous crime, and that the entire world around him will understand it as such—as they will also understand why he had to wipe out his oppressors. Punish him they may, but they will understand. Everyone will.

For a (by now) long line of young killers, this inner assurance has been enough, evidently, to overcome all taboos, all consciousness of what it means to murder, and enough, also, to overcome what would have been, in another time, the most profound inhibition of all—namely fear of what people would think, what friends, teachers and authorities would say of them in the face of an act so unimaginable in its horror.

Charles Andrew Williams could probably have predicted—give or take a detail or two—the comments of friends and teachers. They would speak of their amazement because he didn't seem the type. Some would remember he had been teased. Everyone would look for causes. There would be talk about him, and plenty of it, on television. At the end of a day's reporting on the event it would be hard to find viewers who didn't know who Charles Andrew Williams was. And just as hard to find any who knew the names of the two people Andy killed, the victims in these affairs being, as always, a subject of infinitely small importance compared with the great journey of discovery on which so many media journalists are now embarked as they ask, who is Charles Andrew Williams? What made him tick?

A delicious question and one that Charles Andrew Williams could have predicted everyone would ask after the deed was done—along with a lot of related queries. How had Andy been feeling? How bad was it? Over and over, since [the shooting], press reporters have delivered a rich bounty of answers to this searching question, all of them, of course, the same. He was feeling pretty bad, it seems, what with school bullying. How's that for an answer to the murder of two classmates—Randy Gordon, 17, and Bryan Zuckor, 14—and the wounding of 13 others?

Evidently it was enough to bring forth lengthy meditations on the dangers of school bullying—a subject to which CNN, for one, devoted considerable time. The network news brought reports of a learned study on school bullying, and the Associated Press brings word that the Colorado Legislature is arranging for an antibullying program to be set up in the state's schools. Indeed, a newcomer to this story who tuned in could easily have concluded that it was all about a terrible crime that had taken place in a California school—and that the victim was a youth called Charles Andrew Williams.

3

Violence in Video Games and Other Media Can Cause School Shootings

Paul Keegan

Paul Keegan is a New York–based journalist who has written articles on business technology and culture for Mother Jones, *the* New York Times, *and other publications.*

In the wake of Columbine and other school shootings, many people have argued that video games encourage such violence. Some of the most popular video games have vivid depictions of violence and emphasize that violence in their advertisements. Although the video game industry and many of its fans maintain otherwise, studies suggest that, as with violent movies and television programs, a connection likely exists between brutality in games and real-life aggression. These studies have shown that repeated exposure to violent images can make people less sensitive to the effects of violence. Unless society changes its forms of entertainment, the people playing these games are at risk of becoming isolated from society and resorting to school shootings and other violent acts.

> And shall we just carelessly allow children to hear . . . tales which may be devised by casual persons, and to receive into their minds ideas for the most part the very opposite of those which we should wish them to have when they are grown up?
>
> —Plato, 374 B.C.

Walking down Figueroa Street toward the Los Angeles Convention Center [in 1999], it was impossible to miss the giant white face staring down from a billboard, the eyes glowing bright yellow-orange, the pupils twisted into black spirals. The promotion for the Sega Dreamcast, a new video-game console, was designed to psych up game fans for the zoned-out bliss awaiting them at E3—the Electronic Entertainment Exposition trade show—then getting under way.

Defending the video game industry

But because it appeared just three weeks after the school shootings in Littleton, at a time when video and computer games were emerging as a favorite target of blame, the image suddenly took on new meaning. It succinctly posed the biggest question surrounding the mammoth, $6.3 billion electronic-games industry, now poised to blow past Hollywood in terms of both annual revenue and cultural impact: What's going on behind those eyes?

Images of evil that are destroying our children's minds, cried the critics immediately after it was reported that Eric Harris and Dylan Klebold were avid players of the popular shoot-'em-ups *Doom* and *Quake*. CBS's *60 Minutes* broadcast a segment a few days later asking, "Are Video Games Turning Kids Into Killers?" Bills were introduced on Capitol Hill to ban the sale of violent video games to minors. In June 1999, President Clinton ordered the surgeon general to study the effects of all violent media on children and young adults. He singled out video games in particular, pointing to research showing that half the electronic games a typical seventh-grader plays are violent. "What kind of values are we promoting," chimed in Hillary Clinton, "when a child can walk into a store and find video games where you win based on how many people you can kill or how many places you can blow up?"

Four decades of research . . . have shown a clear correlation between violence on television and the development and display of aggressive values.

The industry launched a counteroffensive, arguing that the vast majority of video games sold today are not violent, and emphasizing that no causal link has ever been established between aggressive behavior and prior exposure to violent media. "The entertainment software industry has no reason to run and hide," said Doug Lowenstein of the Interactive Digital Software Association (IDSA) at E3's opening press conference. He insisted that the simple reason the electronic-games industry is growing twice as fast as the movie business, and four times faster than the recording or book publishing industries, is that they "offer some of the most compelling, stimulating, and challenging entertainment available anywhere, in any form."

And so the E3 love-in carried on as usual this year, with 50,000 people jammed into an enormous exhibition space to sample the hottest new games. But as I wandered through the booths amid a constant roar of car crashes, monster screams, gunfire, and deafening techno-pop soundtracks, I wondered how this industry could have become so wildly popular in some circles and so utterly vilified in others. Is it true, as game developers like to say, that future generations will look back at today's controversy with the kind of bemusement now reserved for those grainy black-and-white images of crew-cutted right-wingers denouncing comic books and rock 'n' roll back in the 1950s? Or do critics have a point in saying that today's media technology has become so powerful and ubiquitous that a laissez-faire attitude toward pop culture is naive and outdated, if not outright dangerous?

Clues to the answers lie within a peculiar subculture of young, white, American males who make up the industry's technological vanguard. But to get a sense of what's behind those swirling eyeballs, first you have to play some games.

The attraction to video games

According to industry ethos, the coolest electronic titles are not video games, which are played on dumbed-down console units made by Sony, Nintendo, and Sega, and account for nearly three-quarters of all game sales. Rather, the cutting edge is occupied by computer games—the other slice of the pie—because they run best on souped-up PCs that allow hardcore fans to customize a game by tinkering with its programming code. Leaving the noisy main hall at E3, I enter a hushed room full of educational PC gaming titles and stop at the Mindscape Entertainment booth to check out the latest version of *Myst*, the best-selling PC title of all time. *Myst* earned its widespread popularity without benefit of rocket launchers or flying body parts. It's a role-playing game that takes place on a bucolic, forested island surrounded by clouds and ocean. The images are beautifully rendered: The forest mist is finely textured, and even the crevices on the tree bark are crisp and clear. The object of the game is to figure out why a team of scientists who were doing research on the island suddenly disappeared.

The game has a stately pace as you click through the foggy pathways and walkways, searching for clues. It's like looking at a series of pretty pictures. But if one thing is clear from spending time at E3, it's that this industry is driven largely by the pursuit of quite a different sensory experience: raw speed. That's true across the board, for the makers of PC games and video games alike. Sony, Nintendo, and Sega—all of which will introduce superpowerful, 128-bit game consoles to the market in the coming year—are not spending billions of dollars to create clever story lines. They are competing madly with one another to create the fastest video-game console ever, each boasting more horsepower than some of the most powerful supercomputers packed just 10 years ago.

Researchers and marketers have known for decades that when it comes to kids and their toys, speed sells. Give a child a choice between a storybook and a television set, and guess which one will grab his attention. "'Sesame Street' learned in the '60s that it's best to change the scene often, move fast, keep the visual display constantly changing," says Professor John Murray, a child psychologist at Kansas State University who has studied the effects of television violence for 30 years. "Very often just the act of playing the game, regardless of content, is what is so engaging."

Myst is a storybook compared to the other games out in the main exhibition hall. There, I could lead a battalion of spaceships through the galaxy, make players dunk basketballs and hit home runs, and drive around a track in a race car. All of these games draw the player's attention because of that sense of moving through space; an appreciation of the rules and subtleties of gameplay come later.

But as thrilling as these games are, something's missing from all of them—something I can't quite put my finger on until I come upon an enormous poster of a guy who looks like an Aryan Nation thug: blond crew cut, open vest, a gun in each hand.

Duke Nukem is one of the bad-boy "first-person shooter" games that have brought such disrepute to the industry. Though shooters represent less than seven percent of overall sales, a recent Time/CNN poll showed that 50 percent of teenagers between 13 and 17 who have played video games have played them. Ten percent say they play regularly. A break-through game will fly off the shelves: Best-selling shooters *Doom* and *Quake* have had combined sales of 4.2 million. (*Myst* and its sequel, *Riven*, top the sales charts at 5.4 million.)

What makes these shooter games so compelling is the addition of freedom of movement to the sensation of speed. This is accomplished by the highly sophisticated underlying technology, called "real-time 3-D." Unlike the "pre-rendered" art of *Myst*—which limits your wanderings to predetermined paths—these images are not created in advance, but rather in "real time," on the fly, with the computer calculating at astronomical rates. Thus you get a euphoric sense of entering a fantastic new world and being able to roam about at breathtaking speeds. That freedom of move-ment is what's missing from the other games out on the floor at E3: The space game didn't let me go inside the ship, and the racing simulation wouldn't even let me get out of the car. Real-time 3-D gives you the illu-sion of maneuvering with no restrictions whatever.

The realism of shooting games

Because real-time 3-D games and their fans stand firmly on the technology's leading edge, they represent a new avant-garde in popular entertainment—in much the same way that innovative independent films have an impact on Hollywood far beyond what their grosses might suggest. In both cases, tastes and techniques formed in one subculture eventually migrate to the broader culture, with enormous impact.

One of the most remarkable new titles is *Quake III Arena*, on display at the id Software booth. The Dallas-based company has perhaps the most advanced game software on the market. The detail in *Quake III Arena* is stunning—you believe you can reach out and touch the stone dungeon walls. Using the mouse, you can look around 360 degrees, which imme-diately makes you feel inside the gorgeous picture you're looking at. Able to go in any direction by pressing the arrow buttons on the keyboard, you instinctively start navigating this strange new universe, learning its laws of physics, mastering its peculiar rules and logic. When you jump from a launching pad located in outer space, it's exhilarating to hurtle through the airless void. This is virtual reality for the masses, on your home com-puter, without goggles or a trip to the arcade.

Calling these experiences "games" understates their significance. They are closer to acid trips, altering your sense of perception in a funda-mental way. Your stomach churns with motion sickness even though you're sitting perfectly still. When you stop playing and stand up, objects in the room swim through space. The clock indicates you've been playing for an hour when you could swear it's been only 10 minutes. Later, driving down the highway, you feel like you are stopped in the middle of the road while cars around you slowly back up.

But *Quake III Arena*, like all shooters, gives you only a few seconds to enjoy the medium before you get the message, loud and clear. As you drop hundreds of feet through space, you notice other inhabitants milling about on the landing platform below. Being a friendly sort, you approach them. Big mistake: They open fire. Reflexively, fearfully, you begin to shoot back. Heads and arms start exploding.

In this magical environment, only one form of social exchange is permitted. The images this astonishing new technology is most often called upon to render so lovingly are rivers of blood and chunks of torn flesh. In a middle-class neighborhood in suburban Dallas, five young guys in their 20s sit on two long, black leather couches. It's an ordinary living room except that the couches do not face each other. They are side-by-side, facing the altar: a video screen big enough to be a clubhouse they could all climb into.

Detached from violence

These guys—"a bunch of kids who like to play games," says Steve Gibson, a skinny 23-year-old with long sideburns, in his soft, slightly embarrassed voice—are living out the fantasy of every hardcore gamer: earning a living making and playing 3-D action games. Steve runs a gaming website called shugashack.com; the rest work at companies that have sprouted up here after the runaway success of id Software's *Doom* and *Quake* in the mid-'90s. As shooter fans, they belong to a largely hidden subculture whose members serve as the ultimate arbiters of cool within the larger electronic-games industry.

They go wild over shooter games not because they are inherently any more bloodthirsty than the average American male—they say they simply love the real-time 3-D programs and the sensations they stimulate. When it comes to "story," they care primarily about allowing the technology to fully express itself—which rules out peaceful adventure games like *Myst* that don't push the technological envelope or provide that crucial adrenaline rush.

Dan, Jack, Steve, Patrick, and Scott are nice guys—smart, courteous, some of them shy, others outgoing—and when they say that blowing away zillions of digital characters since they were kids hasn't made them the least bit aggressive in real life, you believe them.

"You're detached from the violence," explains Dan Hammans, a 19-year-old who, playing under the name Rix, has won several major *Quake* tournaments. "Yeah, saying you like computer games for violence is like saying you like baseball for running," Jack adds. "Violence is there to grab people, get them into it, and have them say, 'That looks cool.' But once you get into it, you don't even notice the violence. You don't go, 'Oh, cool, he blew up!'"

Their comments remind me of Marshall McLuhan's theory that all technology has a certain numbing effect, which he compared with Narcissus' rapture at lake's edge. Though every medium has this narcotic effect, McLuhan argued, modern technology is progressing so fast that we can finally see these changes as if for the first time, "like a growing plant in an enormously accelerated movie."

Researching the link between media violence and aggression

McLuhan uttered his famous dictum—"The medium is the message"—at a time when television was the miraculous new medium, and social scientists focused on the message, which was violence. Today's media experts say the last four decades of research (including a 1972 surgeon general's report) have shown a clear correlation between violence on television and the development and display of aggressive values and behavior by both children and adults.

So there's a statistical correlation. But is there direct proof of cause and effect? "Not only isn't there proof, but there may never be proof," says Kansas State's Murray. But, he continues, "At some point, you have to say that if exposure to violence is related to aggressive attitudes and values, and if [the latter] are related to shooting classmates or acting aggressively—all of which we know to be true—then it stands to reason that there is probably a link between exposure to violence and aggressive actions."

To substantiate this thesis, Murray is turning to physiology. He and a colleague are using functional magnetic resonance imaging to establish that certain areas of the brain controlling "fight-or-flight" impulses are stimulated in kids between the ages of 9 and 12 when they watch violent movies. More surprisingly, they have found, other parts of the brain are affected too—those involving memory and learning. Murray hopes these tests will eventually prove an elusive point: that repeated exposure to violent images is desensitizing, which he defines as having the effect of rendering a person "less sensitive to the pain and suffering of others, and more willing to tolerate ever-increasing levels of violence in our society."

Playing games from the point of view of the killer is making some kids start thinking and acting like assassins.

"The issue people are worried about," Murray says, "is whether repeated rushes of stimulation cause the memory to store away ever-more-violent images, to be recalled later as a possible response to frustration. Are we producing hair-trigger responses and becoming so desensitized that we behave aggressively? Certainly that's what social-science work over the last 40 years has shown—that exposure to [media] violence changes our values, makes us more likely to act out aggressively. Not by viewing a particular program, but [after consuming] a steady diet of violence." There hasn't been much research into the effects of video games, Murray says, and that's not only because they're so new. Many of the experts believe their point has already been proven, as much as humanly possible, with television. "It's a direct translation to video games," says

Murray. "The only thing that's different and more worrisome is that the viewer or player is actively involved in constructing the violence."

According to other critics, playing games from the point of view of the killer is making some kids start thinking and acting like assassins. Lt. Col. Dave Grossman, a former West Point psychology professor, has been appearing on media outlets nationwide to plug his new book, *Stop Teaching Our Kids to Kill* (co-authored with Gloria DeGaetano), and to argue that children are getting the kind of sophisticated military training that until recently only the Pentagon could provide. "For the video game industry to claim that [research on] television and movie violence doesn't apply to them is like saying data on cigarettes doesn't apply to cigars," he says.

All these experts sound convincing until you find yourself in a Dallas living room chatting with five regular guys who play *Quake* long into the night, night after night. The fact that 99.99 percent of the kids who play violent games don't commit murder, they contend, disproves the experts' theories.

And in truth, not only do the games seem utterly harmless on this night, but these guys have so much fun playing together that it's hard to imagine the experience as anything but positive. Their camaraderie is as real as you'll find in any locker room. "It's how geeks get out their competitive spirit," says Steve, "because they're not athletic enough to play on the basketball team."

A game that goes too far

So benign is the mood here that I'm surprised by their reaction to a new game called *Kingpin: Life of Crime*. I fully expect them to draw the line here—for this is a game that goes way over the top with its graphic violence and racial stereotypes. Instead, they laugh and nod their approval at what a great game *Kingpin* is.

Kingpin takes place in a ghetto. As the game starts, you're lying in an alley, having been beaten up by a rival gang. You want revenge, but don't know who to trust. You need guns and money to survive, and quickly learn that the easiest way to do that is to kill people. As you meet people on the street—like this tough, bare-midriffed chick with vaguely ethnic features coming toward you—you're encouraged to talk to them first in case they have any valuable information.

"Shit, man," she says, coming into view, filling up the whole screen. Pressing letters on your keyboard produces either a positive or negative reply. You push the negative key: "Piss off."

"Hey, fuck you too!" she says, not missing a beat. "You a badass motherfucker."

Angry now, you push the negative key again: "You're not talking to me, are you?"

"Now that's it, motherfucker," she says.

"Turn the fuck around," you say. "You fuckin' piece of shit."

"Yeah, fuck you too," she says.

"You fuckin' want some of me?"

"I can get down with yo ass," she says.

"You can fuckin' kiss my ass," you say. "I will fuckin' bury you."

Conversations like this can go on indefinitely in this game until you either walk away or attack with your choice of a wide variety of weapons, including pipes, crowbars, pistols, shotguns, heavy rifles, tommy guns, flamethrowers, and rocket launchers. Not only can you blow off people's legs, arms, or heads, but *Kingpin*'s glossy magazine ads encourage you to do so. "Target specific body parts," the copy screams, "and actually see the damage done—including exit wounds."

Kingpin is rated "M" for mature audiences by the Entertainment Software Rating Board (the voluntary system created by the IDSA), but surveys show that parents don't follow these ratings, and stores don't enforce them. Even if they did, any clever eight-year-old could download a full-featured demo version of the game over the Internet and play all night.

There is something chilling in the number of kids across the country who related deeply . . . to the isolation and alienation of the Columbine killers.

Early reviews among hardcore gamers have been spectacular. "Good is an understatement for *Kingpin*," enthused the now-defunct website 4-Gamers.nu. "Amazing, stunning, and truly awe-inspiring are words which come closer to describing just how joyous this game is."

Separating the medium from the message is not easy when it comes to technologically advanced games like *Kingpin* because the two are so deeply intertwined—its dreamlike, three-dimensional world will vanish unless you learn to kill.

But regardless of whether you prefer McLuhan's theory about the numbing effect of the medium itself, or Murray's belief that desensitization flows from the constant message of mayhem, the result appears to be the same: a gradual increase in our cultural tolerance of violence, one we don't even notice until something shocking and new like *Kingpin* jolts us from our stupor.

Video games and a changing culture

Does that mean today's most gruesome games will eventually become so commonplace that they will elicit nothing more than a bored yawn? That's already happening among today's hardcore gamers, those taste makers who must give a computer game their blessing before it has much chance of migrating to the mainstream video-console market. Which makes hanging out with the Dallas shooter fans a bit like spending time in the future.

The main problem with *Kingpin*'s story is not the violence or the stereotypes, they say, but that it's too self-conscious. "It burned me because it seems like they tried to be shocking," says Jack Mathews, a baby-faced 22-year-old programmer. "Like, 'Look, we're saying "fuck" all the time.' But frankly, the whole game industry is not a very mature industry."

His last comment may reveal the most crucial point: that spending long periods of time absorbed in any medium, especially one as immersive as a video game, can keep you locked safely in a bubble, protected from the real world, in an extended state of arrested development.

Growth, after all, seldom occurs without pain. Is the recent rash of school shootings being caused, at least in part, by the exponential increase in technology's ability to numb pain by drawing kids into an isolated world where violence and aggression have no consequences?

Eugene Provenzo thinks so. The professor of education at the University of Miami, who is writing a book called *Children and Hyperreality: The Loss of the Real in Contemporary Childhood and Adolescence*, believes we're only at the beginning of an evolutionary process—one that has seen the gory comic book of the 1950s evolve first into the slasher movie and now into virtual nightmares like *Kingpin*. "I've been trying hard to make people realize we're going into a very different culture as a result of the introduction of new technologies," says Provenzo. "Video games are extremely powerful teaching machines, and we're still at a primitive level. We're on a trajectory toward increasing realism, or hyperreality, that makes people start thinking they can shoot someone and it doesn't hurt, that they can recover."

Cultural critics like Provenzo see evidence that the damaging effects of this phenomenon are hardly limited to a few crackpot shooters in remote places like Jonesboro and Paducah. And there is something chilling in the number of kids across the country who related deeply not only to the isolation and alienation of the Columbine killers, but to the way they vented their anger.

"My social studies teacher asked if we wanted to talk about Littleton," one high school kid in Illinois wrote in an e-mail posted recently on a website called Slashdot (its slogan: "News for nerds"). "I said I had some sense of how those two kids might have been driven crazy by cruel students, since it happens to me. I said I had thought of taking my father's gun to school when I was in the ninth grade and was so angry." That was among thousands of e-mails received in the wake of Littleton by new-media columnist Jon Katz, now writing a book called *Geeks*. Katz wrote movingly on Slashdot about how self-described "geeks, nerds, dorks, and goths" were singled out for abuse by teachers and schoolmates after the Columbine massacre (the Illinois teenager who spoke so freely in class, in fact, came home to find three detectives going through his room); in follow-up postings they told horrible stories of being punched and kicked, tied up and beaten, and otherwise abused and humiliated. Pleas for help by these outcast kids instantly became part of the national dialogue, being entered into the *Congressional Record*, reprinted in the *New York Times* and *Los Angeles Times*, and read aloud on National Public Radio.

"The interesting thing about Littleton is that it was the first time the country realized there is this culture out there," says Provenzo. "It's not happening in the cities—it's an alienation we've created in suburbs and small towns, and it's being aggravated by a whole series of media formats. Our kids are losing their handle on reality because of everything from malls to video games. Each thing may be a drop in the bucket, but the bucket is full."

Acknowledging the effects of video games

The computer-gamers gathered in the Dallas living room say they feel as though they don't hear enough about the evils of other media—which, they point out, are far more politically powerful and entrenched than the electronic-games industry. "When people see stuff [like Littleton] happen, they say, 'Oh, these computer freaks! Look at them, they're freaks!'" says Jack. "But when people see violence on TV, creatures exploding and people running around shooting with a shotgun, it's okay."

Dan acknowledges that what he loves about playing is that feeling of "being in another world with no consequences of your actions. You can jump off a ledge and smack on the ground and enjoy it." But there's a crystal-clear distinction in their minds between fantasy and real life, they add quickly, and for much of the evening they argue that spending so much time in their virtual worlds doesn't affect them at all.

At one point, though, Dan slips up.

"I've been walking around in a grocery store and swore I heard grenades bouncing around," he says. "Weird things like that—when you spend so much time doing it and [then] you hear a similar noise. . . ."

"Man!" cries Jack, interrupting him. "That's going to make it in the [magazine] now! 'These crazy game players!' 'Dan says he hears grenades while he walks around!'"

"No," Dan protests. "What I'm trying to say is there's no correlation between—" He stops. Some of their employers, afraid of being sued by the families of school-shooting victims, have instructed them not to discuss the issue of electronic games and its relationship to violent behavior/

Will we simply return to a fantasy world where we can pretend that the ways we choose to entertain ourselves have no consequences?

Dan starts over. "It's so obvious to anybody who plays the game," he says. "You're running around in the game and you've got a shotgun, but it's a 3-D model being rendered by the game, and there's just no way I could see anybody not being able to tell the difference." Later, just to be sure the point is clear, Dan adds, "It doesn't transfer over to reality—that's the biggest thing."

But how could it not? If media doesn't affect real-world behavior, there would be no such thing as advertising, which at last count was a $25 billion international business. Exactly how it affects us depends on the person, of course, and the effect can be quite subtle. But arguing that these games have no effect at all is absurd, given that everybody in this room is devoting his life to developing increasingly powerful ways of fooling your mind and body into believing the game experience is really happening to you.

I have one last question for these guys. Isn't there anything else they would like to do in their miraculous virtual worlds besides killing people and blowing things up?

"It's more fun to blow up things than to build things," explains Dan.

Jack shrugs. "Violence sells."

It's years in the future. French terrorists have launched an attack on the Statue of Liberty, and you—a new agent in the United Nations Anti-Terrorist Coalition—have been sent to stop them. What you don't realize yet is that your employers are using you as a guinea pig in a nanotechnology experiment. You are fully equipped with a range of weapons—everything from knives and pepper spray to rifles and rocket launchers. But here's the twist: You have to think twice before blowing people away.

"If you shoot somebody and anybody hears it, alarms are going to go off and the police are going to be all over you," says Warren Spector. The developer for Ion Storm, a Texas-based gaming software company, is standing in front of his booth at E3 excitedly describing the new game he's creating, called *Deus Ex,* due out next year. "People who would have talked to you before won't talk to you anymore. You'll still be able to win the game—I don't want to be disingenuous about this—but I want the player to be able to make a choice and then to really see the consequences of that choice. So suddenly we're in a medium that isn't just about adrenaline rushes."

Spector is part of a small band of game developers working in real-time 3-D who are quite literally trying to separate the medium from the message. He licensed the software program that runs a popular first-person shooter called *Unreal,* extracted most of the shooting gameplay, and is creating a new virtual universe that bears a closer resemblance to the real world, with some of its moral complexities and hard choices.

But Spector is the first to admit that his new game probably won't sell nearly as well as the gory shooters. And why should it? Who wants a fantasy that holds you responsible for your actions? Isn't that the whole point of American entertainment—to provide an escape from reality? Whether games like *Deus Ex* manage to succeed in the marketplace against the likes of *Quake* and *Kingpin* should provide some clues as to whether interactive entertainment is ready to take any tentative steps toward acknowledging what goes on in the real world.

The stakes are high, say social critics like Eugene Provenzo, who believes that our embrace of electronic games represents nothing less than a massive renegotiation with reality, with profound implications for how kids, in particular, learn about and understand the world. As supercomputers and expanding band-width change passive television into an interactive medium that can draw us into the most astonishing simulated worlds, we are nearing a crossroads at least as important as the moment flickering television images began transforming the American cultural landscape in the '50s.

It was decades before the effects of television were broadly debated—by which time screen violence was something kids simply took for granted as a normal part of childhood. We have the chance to do things differently this time, but it may require discussions more imaginative than the usual free-market versus government-control polemics. Entertainers from Snoop Doggy Dogg to network-cop-show producers have eased up on the brutality lately, and consumers seem more open to the possibility that today's mass media may be creating public health problems as severe as those caused by our disruption of the natural environment during the last great technological revolution.

But a question remains: Now that the shock of Littleton has subsided, will we simply return to a fantasy world where we can pretend that the ways we choose to entertain ourselves have no consequences, like some kid zoned out in front of a computer game? If so, game's over.

4

Violence in the Media Does Not Lead to School Shootings

Barbara Dority

Barbara Dority is executive director of the Washington Coalition Against Censorship (WCAC), the president of the Humanists of Washington, editor of the Secular Humanist Press, *and a columnist for the* Humanist *magazine.*

Despite what many commentators claim, studies have not found a causal link between violence in the media and school shootings. Although many adolescents play video games that feature simulated violence, incidents of school violence have actually decreased over the past decade. Alternative lifestyles, including the Goth movement, are also wrongfully associated with school shootings. The common solutions to school shootings, such as metal detectors, increased police presence, and bans on certain types of clothing, are simple-minded and ignore the real problems facing children, including poverty and lack of child care.

Columbine High School is an open, attractive, sprawling campus in the middle of a relatively safe suburban enclave in Littleton, Colorado. The school was a showplace when it opened, distinguishing itself in academics, music, drama, and athletics. Thus it was an unlikely setting for a tragedy of the magnitude that took place on April 20, 1999, when witnesses say at least two students—eighteen-year-old Eric Harris and seventeen-year-old Dylan Klebold—killed thirteen people and wounded twenty-three others before shooting themselves.

Fellow students later said the group Harris and Klebold belonged to, self-proclaimed the Trench Coat Mafia, had been a target of derision for at least four years. Members were picked on, harassed, and excluded— "always on the outside looking in." Most of the time, the members appeared to like it that way. As many cliques of young people do, the members played up their differentness. They wore army gear, black trench coats, and Nazi symbols. They spoke German to each other and were

Reprinted, with permission, from "The Columbine Tragedy: Countering the Hysteria," by Barbara Dority, *The Humanist*, July 1999.

quite vocal about their fascination with Hitler and World War II.

Membership in such groups is just one of a remarkable assortment of "explanations" and assignments of blame that panicked overreaction to this tragedy has produced, accompanied by an onslaught of repressive "solutions" allegedly designed to prevent recurrences. We are witnessing the institution of a myriad of alarming civil-liberties violations, most aimed at obstructing the basic rights of young people—an already heavily restricted group of U.S. citizens.

This is a classic scenario: particularly shocking incidents of violence, especially those involving young people, lead to mass hysteria and are invariably used to justify repressive government intervention. Fred Medway, psychology professor at the University of South Carolina, says, "People feel much more comfortable overreacting than underreacting. It makes them feel they've done something to prevent a potentially negative thing from happening."

The reality of school violence

It is in the midst of just such frightening and dangerous times that this tendency to overreact must be most forcefully resisted. A few reality checks can be the first step in countering panic and assisting us in putting the situation into a realistic perspective:

• According to information from the National School Safety Center, killings are the exception, not the rule, at schools across the United States, and suburban and rural schools remain safer than their inner-city counterparts.

• The number of violent deaths in both urban and suburban neighborhoods has dropped dramatically since 1992. More than 95 percent of children are never involved in a violent crime.

• Not one of the mass school shootings of the past two and a half years has occurred in an inner-city area, and nearly all victims have been white.

• A 1998 report by the U.S. Departments of Justice and Education says children have more chance of getting killed by lightning than suffering a violent death on campus—which boils down to less than one chance in a million.

• The current generation of teenagers is less likely to use drugs, more sexually conservative, and less likely to be caught up in school violence than the one of twenty years ago.

• It's not unusual for young males, especially students at large suburban schools, to make videos of shootings and robberies in video-production classes (as Harris and Klebold are said to have done); in fact, nearly half do so.

• In a recent survey of 900 fourth- through eighth-grade students, almost half said their favorite video games involve simulated violence.

• High-profile school violence isn't new. Similar incidents have occurred at least as early as the 1950s.

Blaming the media

But despite all these facts, we're being told that the primary cause of the Columbine and similar tragedies is violence on network television and in cartoons, comic books, music, and movies. As usual, Hollywood is to blame. Next in line are various "violent" games, especially "killing" video games and "violent" toys.

✒ And, of course, we must not forget that wildly dangerous and insidious corruptor of American youth: the Internet—where Harris and Klebold are said to have gotten their bomb-making knowledge. It must be noted, however, that such terrorist know-how, complete with illustrated instructions for making bombs, is also frequently available in military manuals at surplus stores, as well as in numerous mail-order civilian manuals, which are available through some public libraries. Are proponents of censoring this information advocating that we somehow locate, remove, and destroy all these sources?

Nation columnist Alexander Cockburn addresses a closely related aspect of public reaction in the magazine's May 17, 1999, issue:

> Commentators have fastened onto the fact that one of the youths had a personal Web site "espousing an addled philosophy of violence." Those were the words of the *New York Times'* [editorial team, the same people] who espoused an addled philosophy of violence a few days earlier when they suggested that NATO intensify the bombing of Serbia. Perhaps . . . it wasn't a personal Web site the kid had in his computer but nytimes.com.

I'm not, of course, insinuating that the war in Yugoslavia caused the Columbine tragedy or any other instances of domestic crime. I am, however, appalled at the hypocrisy of those who blame such incidents on the media and popular culture while simultaneously ignoring violence perpetrated by our own government.

They ignore, too, that the institution most adept at putting guns into the hands of youngsters (many of them troubled) and training them to kill their fellow human beings is, of course, the U.S. military—which also insists on the right to accept teenagers at an age younger than most other nations. It is amazing that those who are now blaming media violence for the Columbine tragedy—President Clinton among them—can completely exclude sanctioned, even glorified violence of this magnitude from their analysis. Yet, clearly they can and do fail to realize that, in order to maintain consistency and credibility, they must equally condemn all violence. This incredible feat of dissociation by government officials and the American public is so complete that no one noticed the appalling irony when the Air Force sent F-16s over the funerals for those killed in Littleton.

In reality, and contrary to thousands of news sources, absolutely no causal link has been established between simulated violence in media and actual real-life violence. Just one example of how the media blatantly misrepresents this issue can be found in an Associated Press story that appeared a few days after the Littleton incident. It was picked up by most major newspapers under various versions of the headline, "Scores of studies link media and youth violence." The story opens by referring to a bill in Congress to require the U.S. surgeon general to conduct a comprehensive study of the effects of media violence on American youths, then immediately goes on to state that "the evidence already exists." Finally, five paragraphs into the story, we read that "a few scholars object to this research, saying the links do not prove cause and effect."Among those who object is Jonathan Freedman, professor of psychology at the University of Toronto. He points out that correlative links could come from many factors, including the likelihood that children who watch a lot of violent television are often those least supervised by responsible adults. Freedman tries repeatedly to make the simple point most researchers recognize: that correlations don't establish causal links. Harvard psychiatrist James Gilligan, who spent years interviewing murderers in Massachusetts, has concluded, "Nothing stimulates violence as powerfully as the experience of being shamed and humiliated." Still, one after another, congressional representatives continue to pronounce that simulated violence produced by Hollywood is to blame for violence in our society. They then threaten government intervention to curb violence in movies, video games, and music if this is not done "voluntarily." Republican Senator Orrin Hatch of Utah and Democratic Senator Joseph Lieberman of Connecticut have likened the content of popular entertainment to a vice industry, claiming that, like tobacco, it requires special attention on public-safety grounds.

For all but a tiny percentage of young people [video games] serve as a means of blowing off steam.

The April 28 edition of *20/20* presented a particularly shameless and sensationalistic feature about a "violent movement" spreading across America to which Harris and Klebold supposedly belonged. The followers of this new movement, Sam Donaldson grimly reported, call themselves "Goths." This feature then proceeded to demonize and place blame for violence on the Gothic American subculture. Parents were told that "warning signs" include being "attracted to a very strange group of people and listening to very alternative music." Diane Sawyer then haphazardly lumped together music groups with very little in common. As was the case with many of the music groups that various news sources connected with the Columbine suspects, most of them don't even fit the Goth mold. In fact, the boys themselves didn't fit any known Goth mold. Neither did their lifestyles. And never mind that the modern Goth lifestyle dates back to the 1970s. "What they're thinking," warned the Denver Police Department's Steve Rickard in the *20/20* report, "is totally irrelevant to a normal person's thoughts." What does this say about the many thousands of young professionals who grew up listening to Goth music, who solved video games like *Doom* and *Quake* years ago, and who once participated in the grandfather of all supposedly mind-warping games, *Dungeons and Dragons*? If *20/20* is to be believed, most of us are surrounded by ticking time bombs.

The obvious appeal of "very alternative" music, like many other forms of pop music, is that it gives voice to feelings of loneliness or anger shared by many young people and usually serves as an outlet for these feelings. Out-of-the-mainstream lifestyles, complete with music, provide a vital form of release. Many other seemingly anti-social behaviors are part of the rebellion we've come to accept as a normal and healthy part of the maturation process. Usually kids outgrow its self-destructive and counterproductive aspects. Similarly, although many video games do feature virtual guns and carnage, for all but a tiny percentage of young people they serve as a means of blowing off steam, certainly not as a blueprint for actual killing.

In the past twenty years, the Goth subculture has become its own culture, generating many subcultures within itself. I am acquainted with several young people who are part of this. They share my concern at the media's portrayal of Harris and Klebold as Goths. Several have been harassed on the street since the Columbine incident. Yet the truth is that violence is anathema to most Gothic lifestyles. And Nazism is not glorified by Goths. How could it be, my friends ask, when Goths would be among the first persecuted by Nazis today? They fear for younger "quiet freaks" still in high school "who wear black, tint their hair, have multiple piercings, write dark poetry—and aren't ever going to hurt anyone." So do I. My Goth friends also point out that there are many more computer and video game players in much of Asia than in the United States, and we don't hear about similar incidents in that part of the world. Video games, they say, are fun, and they're just games: "It's what we do for entertainment, what we like, and that's all it is."

A growing police presence

On the front page of my May 2, 1999, newspaper was an eight-by-ten-inch color photograph of four police officers in the main foyer of a local high school. Some are seen talking to students, others are standing guard, and so on. Certainly I've no problem with students meeting and relating to police officers. But students becoming used to seeing police constantly monitoring their normal daily activities? How will this experience affect their perceptions and expectations of privacy? Many are so frightened they welcome this police presence, but what are the implications of creating citizens who feel safe only when directly watched over and protected by law enforcement personnel?

We're also instituting SWAT training in schools; installing metal detectors; conducting random locker searches (these have been mandated for all schools in the Seattle, Washington, school district, along with metal-detector checks in classrooms and at sports events); supplying teachers with walkie-talkies; banning black clothing, symbols of any kind, and any type of trench coat; mandating school uniforms; searching students' backpacks, purses, and such; banning the production of "gruesome" videos in school video classes; and conducting "lock-down drills."

One proposed "solution" to the school violence problem that is enjoying a surge of support is the concept of prosecuting parents for teenagers' crimes (which does seem particularly ridiculous when in most states, until now, any eighteen-year-old could purchase a gun-show pistol immediately). Twenty-three states have extended some form of legal sanctions against parents whose children commit crimes, although rarely are these enforced. Thirteen states now have laws making parents criminally responsible for failing to supervise delinquent children—but, again, rarely are such charges brought. Five states have adopted laws threatening parents with fines or imprisonment for negligent parenting, although some have been struck down by the courts.

All these simplistic solutions avoid confronting the much more difficult problems affecting children, like reducing poverty, improving child-rearing skills, and funding child-care services. Bruce Shapiro, writing in the May 17, 1999, *Nation*, states that "only a broadly conceived community safety net—derided as bleeding-heart social work by those now rushing to blame the culture—can catch such children as they fall." Finally, there is one particular aspect of the American public's reaction to this tragedy that cries out for rational evaluation by freethinkers, as it is rooted in the irrationality of religion. We are subjected to pronouncements that the cause of Columbine and other violent episodes in schools is "Godless parenting" and "America's spiritual drift." Syndicated columnist Donna Britt actually wrote, "Kids grounded in God often have more spiritual weapons with which to fight darkness." The beliefs of Christian kids, she maintains, "get media attention only when awfulness is done in His name."

Christianity was not targeted

When I opened my newspaper on April 27 to the headline "Deaths seen through prism of Christianity," I felt a chill. "How much worse can it get?" I asked myself. I discovered that several of the murdered students were eulogized at funerals and memorial services as "Christian martyrs." Friends and family were quoted expressing how glad they were that these "strong Christians" had the privilege of dying for their belief in Jesus Christ. This is almost incomprehensible.

Unflinchingly facing reality has never been more critical. There is no evidence that Christians or those who believed in God were selectively murdered. The Reverend Barry Palser, minister at the church of one of these Christian martyrs, was quoted as saying, "Inside that school library, they knew what they were doing. They knew what they were going after. That's what Hitler did." What planet are we on here? If these murderers had been adherents of Hitler's doctrines, they would have embraced Christianity and murdered only Jews, atheists, and others outside their faith.

Christians are certainly free to comfort themselves with the fantasy that some of these youngsters were "Christians who died for their beliefs" and to "thank God" they got to go out as "martyrs." But it's just another delusion to avoid dealing with the simple truth: twelve beautiful young people and their teacher were in the wrong place at the wrong time, died tragically and needlessly, and are gone forever.

The even less appealing truth is that we don't know why the murderers did what they did. We don't know why other incidents of school violence have occurred. We don't know if any one incident is meaningfully related to any other, or which incidents, if any, are related to which of a variety of factors in our society. Nor do we know how to prevent future incidents. We certainly can and should continue sincere efforts to learn as much as we can, but we're a long way from any definitive answers. As we await further information from law enforcement officials, it is our task—indeed, our duty as citizens—to resist panicked responses and stand in opposition to such tragedies being used to rationalize draconian violations of young peoples' civil liberties.

5

Access to Guns Can Lead to School Shootings

Evan Gahr

Evan Gahr is a senior fellow at the Hudson Institute and a columnist whose work has appeared in the Washington Post *and* American Enterprise.

Conservatives oppose gun control while advocating laws against drug use. If conservatives were consistent in their philosophy, they would acknowledge that access to guns poses a greater threat to teenagers than the availability of drugs. Emotionally volatile teenagers, such as Charles Andy Williams, who allegedly killed two students at his California high school, pose a danger when they are able to acquire firearms.

Georgia Republican Bob Barr refuses to concede any ground in our nation's war on drugs. In 1999, Representative Barr tried to block implementation of a District of Columbia referendum to allow the seriously ill to use marijuana for medicinal purposes. In retaliation, Barr's office was besieged by angry protesters, including a multiple sclerosis sufferer who said she relieved her pain by adding marijuana to her salad. Barr saw this as one more salvo in a campaign to "make dangerous, mind-altering drugs legally available."

But Barr doesn't tackle all wars with the same determination. Like many other Republicans, Barr is committed to maintaining Americans' easy access to guns. In the wake of the Columbine massacre two years ago, he helped fellow Republicans thwart efforts by congressional Democrats to raise the legal purchase age for guns from 18 to 21. He opposed requiring trigger locks, and, more recently, he railed against requiring a three-day waiting period for weapons purchased at gun shows.

A conservative contradiction

Far from regarding Barr as the extremist that many in Washington dub him, I sympathize with his views and admire his strong stance on drugs.

Reprinted, by permission of the author, from "Fellow Conservatives: Our Position Is Hypocritical," by Evan Gahr, *The Washington Post*, Outlook section, April 22, 2001.

But recently I have come to see him as typifying a dangerous kind of GOP hypocrisy. As a fellow conservative, I find myself asking: Why is the drug war worth fighting at an estimated $60 billion annually, while far more modest measures to keep weapons from criminals and emotionally volatile teenagers are doomed to failure? When I tried to find out from Barr, his office did not respond, leaving me with a basic philosophical problem: Conservatives seem prepared to play John Stuart Mill on guns one minute and William Bennett on drugs the next.

It was *New York Post* columnist Andrea Peyser who first brought this contradiction to my attention last month after 15-year-old student Charles Andrew Williams, armed with his father's .22 caliber revolver and some 40 rounds of ammunition, allegedly killed two students and wounded 13 others at his California high school. Who was the last teenager to massacre his classmates with a bong, I wondered? Don't misunderstand me: Drug use is bad. But can anyone seriously dispute that guns are a far more immediate and dangerous threat?

The conservatives to whom I turned to explain this contradiction have refused to consider any additional gun control measures whatsoever. Let's take a closer look at their arguments:

• Gun control laws are worthless. Several prominent conservatives—including veteran cultural warrior Phyllis Schlafly, whose stance on many issues I admire—noted that we already have 20,000 gun laws on the books. If these laws haven't prevented school shootings, this line of reasoning goes, new measures are simply doomed to failure. Besides, Schlafly writes, "the sheer number of guns and gun owners in America makes gun control far more unrealistic than Prohibition. At least 80 million Americans own about 250 million guns."

Drug use is bad. But can anyone seriously dispute that guns are a far more immediate and dangerous threat?

However, the fact that drug use is so prevalent (37 percent of high school seniors last year told University of Michigan researchers that they had smoked pot within the previous 12 months; 8.2 percent had used the stimulant Ecstasy) does nothing to slow the drug war. Indeed, Attorney General John Ashcroft finds widespread use an argument for greater enforcement. Days after taking office, he vowed on "Larry King Live" to "escalate the war on drugs . . . relaunch it if you will." But he said, "I think we've got enough laws on the books [for guns]."

• Laws do more harm than good. The conservative line is that gun laws are counterproductive. That's right: Guns don't kill people, gun laws do. To prove their point, Schlafly and others fall back on studies done by Yale University scholar John Lott, who claims that in 15 states—including California—tighter gun laws coincided with an increase in crime. And if laws don't work, this line of reasoning goes, let's abandon the fight. Gee, where have I heard this argument before? Ah, yes, from folks determined to abandon the War on Drugs. (You know them, the libertarian crowd whom social conservatives regard as foolish naysayers.) Just last month, the Center for National Policy released a new study, "The War on Drugs: Do the American People Have Battle Fatigue?"

• The family is at fault. Thomas Roeser, a radio talk-show host in Chicago, voiced a classic conservative rationale when he said that "the shootings on the campuses are a result of wide-scale disorientation on the part of families. . . . You can talk all you want about curtailing guns, but that's silly. It's as silly as curtailing knives or any other instrument that can [wound]." Barr echoed this sort of thinking when he said that future "tragedies" could more easily be avoided if all schools prominently displayed the Ten Commandments.

The dangerous consequences of access to guns

But if the sorry state of family life renders concerns about access to guns irrelevant, what about drugs? Why aren't conservatives prepared to throw in the towel in the war on drugs until the two-parent family again becomes our country's norm?

• We need to understand the root causes [of school violence]. Thomas Jipping, director of the Free Congress Foundation's Center for Law and Democracy, is among those who argue that it is time to find out what is behind the dramatic acts of gun violence. "We've got to look at why some young people look at a handgun and yawn. And others look at a handgun and want to pick it up and shoot somebody."

Wait. Don't conservatives generally sneer at calls to place criminals under a sociological microscope? It's usually liberals who want to examine criminal behavior this way. Remember how Rep. Maxine Waters (D-Calif.) blamed poverty and racism for the 1992 Los Angeles riots? Now, though, every school shooting spawns root-cause conservatives. And if we are going to examine those root causes, what about the root causes of drug use?

The nation suffers innumerable consequences from easy access to guns and drugs. Both liberals and conservatives would do well to argue their respective cases strictly on the legal issues (the Second Amendment for guns, right to privacy for drugs). But let's dispense with selective fatalism.

Hey, Bob Barr and friends: How about one standard for both plagues? Or do you want to play enabler for the next Charles Andrew Williams?

6

Guns Have Been Wrongfully Blamed for School Shootings

Dave Kopel and Ari Armstrong

Dave Kopel is the author of numerous books and articles on gun control. He is also the research director for the Independence Institute, an associate policy analyst with the Cato Institute, and the director of the Center on the Digital Economy at the Heartland Institute. Ari Armstrong is the publisher of the Colorado Freedom Report.

The media blame access to guns for school shootings instead of examining the role that parents and gun control have played in these crimes. The parents of these shooters often pay little attention to their children's lives, and their lack of responsibility should be acknowledged. For example, the parents of Charles Andrew Williams, the alleged perpetrator of the shootings at Santana High School in Santee, California, in March 2001, were unaware of his activities and emotional problems. Politicians need to take into consideration parental responsibility when trying to develop legislation that will reduce incidents of school shootings. However, legislators in California and elsewhere persist in approving laws that prevent law-abiding citizens from having access to guns. Instead of reducing violence, California gun laws have led to an increase in homicide and other violent crimes. The media and society as a whole should realize that gun ownership can help prevent or stymie school shootings.

Sure, blame the gun.

Never mind that many students in government schools are routinely tormented and attacked in ways that would constitute a felony (if a school principal, rather than a ninth-grader, were the victim). Often, schools are so big and impersonal that administrators frequently don't even know there's a problem. Or schools may be so sports-focused that athletes can get away with anything.

Reprinted, with permission, from "Sure, Blame the Gun," by Dave Kopel and Ari Armstrong, *National Review Online*, March 9, 2001. Copyright © 2001 by National Review, Inc., National Review Online, www.nationalreview.com.

The Santee, California, murderer (we won't mention his name, because he doesn't deserve the publicity he sought) lived with his father; his mother lives on the other side of the continent. She is reported to have called the young man earlier this year. The killer's former girlfriend said that the killer craved his mother's attention, but never got it. The mother is so minimally aware of her child that she thought he played on all the sports teams. In fact, he played on no team sports.

The killer's father apparently didn't realize his son had severe social and emotional problems, didn't realize that maybe he shouldn't have access to the keys to the gun safe.

But it's the gun's fault—couldn't possibly have anything to do with parental responsibility.

Sure, blame the gun. Keep on ducking real responsibility for children's safety and moral education.

The killer told an adult and several students he was going to shoot up the school. They did nothing. Blame the gun.

California politicians have passed some of the toughest gun laws in the nation. There's government permission and registration for every gun transfer—even giving an old squirrel rifle to your cousin. There are bans on hundreds of cosmetically incorrect firearms; no permits to carry a handgun for lawful protection—unless you've got special political connections; and laws requiring guns to be locked up to keep them away from people like the Santee murderer.

Gun laws do not save lives

So why is California one of the most dangerous states in the Union? Don't all those laws targeting law-abiding gun owners save lives?

The problem with California gun laws in general, and California's mandatory gun storage law in particular, is that they affect precisely the wrong people.

If a father doesn't notice that his son, who is making death threats to everyone who will listen, has swiped a revolver, a mandatory gun-lock law like California's isn't going to stir him into action. On the other hand, responsible parents who obey the law and teach their children to do the same will obey the gun-lock law. These people weren't going to commit crimes with their firearms. Because of the gun-lock laws, these people end up becoming easy prey for criminals.

In Merced, California, in August 2000, a pitchfork-wielding man attacked and murdered Jessica Carpenter's 7-year-old brother and 9-year-old sister while their parents were not home. Jessica's father kept a gun in the home that was, in accordance with California law, locked in a safe. According to the family, Jessica, age 14, is a very good shot, and had the gun not been securely stored, Jessica would have been able to retrieve it and use it to fend off the murderer.

The California mandatory gun-lock law helped kill two children in

Merced. That same law did nothing to save the two children in Santee.

The Merced incident may have been sensational, but it is typical of how laws like California's turn a family's home into a safe zone for predators. A John Lott and John Whitley study compared crime, accident, and suicide trends in states with California-type laws, to trends in other states, while controlling for the effect of numerous sociological variables. The study found no statistically significant reduction in accidents involving children or teenagers. Teenage gun suicide decreased, but not the overall teenage-suicide rate.

There were also large increases in violent crime and homicide:

> Rapes, robberies, and burglaries rise by 9, 11, and 6 percent, respectively, as a result of safe storage laws. . . . The fifteen states with safe storage laws would be expected to experience 168 more murders in the first full year that the law is in effect. The number of murders peaks in the fourth full year at 380 murders. . . . During the five full years after the passage of the safe storage laws, the fifteen states face an annual average increase of 309 more murders, 3,860 more rapes, 24,650 more robberies, and over 25,000 more aggravated assaults.

The media ignores the truth

The crime increase was most severe in states like California, where violation is a felony. But the victims of the California gun lock law never made the national news. And did you read about the four California children who were killed last week by a sociopath who ran them down with an automobile? Of course not. The media's interest in dead children depends mostly on whether those children can be exploited to promote bigger government.

So don't expect a lot of editorial cartoons criticizing parents who expect schools to raise their children. Don't expect too many congressmen with 100% voting records from Handgun Control, Inc., to give a big speech worrying that so many parents spend less than five minutes a day talking with their children. Blame the gun.

A small but terrifying subculture of America's children worship the Columbine murderers. Do you think that *Time* regrets putting the two killers on its cover? Do you think the national media considers for a second how many lives might be saved by simply refusing to broadcast the names of publicity-seeking mass murderers? Do you think the media has the slightest regret for the saturation coverage given the Santee murder, and the three copycat crimes that followed within 48 hours? Blame the gun. Why exercise First Amendment rights in a responsible manner, when it's easier to demonize the Second Amendment?

Upon hearing the shots at Santana High School, one student grabbed a still camera and another grabbed a video camera to record the carnage. No one tried to tackle the killer during his three reloading breaks. Is it because the national media failed to tell the story of the heroic high-school student who tackled the killer in Springfield, Oregon, while the killer was reloading?

The killer became nationally famous. The hero didn't. The media lost interest in him when they found that the hero's father belonged to the NRA, and the family opposed gun control.

At Columbine, teacher Dave Sanders was justifiably lionized for dying while trying to help students flee. Most people have never heard about the adults who saved lives in Pearl, Mississippi, or Edinboro, Pennsylvania, by confronting and subduing the rampaging killers.

To the national media, civilians who take forceful action—wrestling a shooter to the ground, or pointing a handgun at the shooter's head— apparently teach the wrong lesson: that we're not all helpless; that brave people can stop criminals. That's a lesson which conflicts with the enraged helplessness promoted by the "Million" Mom March and its mean-spirited message that the only way for children to be safe is for the government to crack down on law-abiding gun owners.

Sure, blame the gun. Keep on ducking real responsibility for children's safety and moral education. Teach people to be afraid, but not how to protect themselves. Keep on hating inanimate objects and the law-abiding people who own them.

7

Ignoring the Problems of White Teenagers Causes School Shootings

Tim Wise

Tim Wise is a race relations activist and a writer whose work appears regularly in Z Magazine.

White American society refuses to acknowledge that its children are the ones responsible for school shootings. The media encourage this belief by ignoring the race of the shooters in their analyses of the massacres. The unwillingness of white parents to recognize the problems facing white adolescents, including higher rates of drug use than their African-American peers, has prevented society from taking steps to reduce the number of these violent incidents.

I can think of no other way to say this, so here goes: white people need to pull our heads out of our collective ass.

Two more white children are dead and thirteen are injured, and another "nice" community is scratching its blonde head, utterly perplexed at how a school shooting the likes of the one [in March 2001] in Santee, California could happen. After all, as the Mayor of the town said in an interview with CNN: "We're a solid town, a good town, with good kids, a good church-going town, an All-American town." Yeah, well maybe that's the problem.

Ignoring the danger

I said this after Columbine and no one listened so I'll say it again: white people live in an utter state of self-delusion. We think danger is black, brown and poor, and if we can just move far enough away from "those people" in the cities we'll be safe. If we can just find an "All-American" town, life will be better, because "things like this just don't happen here."

Well bullshit on that. In case you hadn't noticed, "here" is about the only place these kinds of things do happen. Oh sure, there is plenty of violence in urban communities and schools. But mass murder; wholesale

Reprinted, with permission, from "School Shootings and White Denial," by Tim Wise, *The Pride* (California State University, San Marcos), March 27, 2001.

slaughter; take-a-gun-and-see-how-many-you-can-kill kinda craziness seems made for those safe places: the white suburbs or rural communities.

And yet once again, we hear the FBI insist there is no "profile" of a school shooter. Come again? White boy after white boy after white boy, with very few exceptions to that rule (and none in the mass shooting category), decides to use their classmates for target practice, and yet there is no profile? Imagine if all these killers had been black: would we still hesitate to put a racial face on the perpetrators? Doubtful.

Indeed, if any black child in America—especially in the mostly white suburbs of Littleton, or Santee—were to openly discuss their plans to murder fellow students, as happened both at Columbine and now Santana High, you can bet your ass that somebody would have turned them in, and the cops would have beat a path to their doorstep. But when whites discuss their murderous intentions, our stereotypes of what danger looks like cause us to ignore it—they're just "talking" and won't really do anything. How many kids have to die before we rethink that nonsense? How many dazed and confused parents, mayors and sheriffs do we have to listen to, describing how "normal" and safe their community is, and how they just can't understand what went wrong?

Listen up my fellow white Americans: your children are no better, no nicer, no more moral, no more decent than anyone else.

I'll tell you what went wrong and it's not TV, rap music, video games or a lack of prayer in school. What went wrong is that white Americans decided to ignore dysfunction and violence when it only affected other communities, and thereby blinded themselves to the inevitable creeping of chaos which never remains isolated too long. What affects the urban "ghetto" today will be coming to a Wal-Mart near you tomorrow, and unless you address the emptiness, pain, isolation and lack of hope felt by children of color and the poor, then don't be shocked when the support systems aren't there for your kids either.

What went wrong is that we allowed ourselves to be lulled into a false sense of security by media representations of crime and violence that portray both as the province of those who are anything but white like us. We ignore the warning signs, because in our minds the warning signs don't live in our neighborhood, but across town, in that place where we lock our car doors on the rare occasion we have to drive there. That false sense of security—the result of racist and classist stereotypes—then gets people killed. And still we act amazed.

But listen up my fellow white Americans: your children are no better, no nicer, no more moral, no more decent than anyone else. Dysfunction is all around you, whether you choose to recognize it or not.

Rethinking stereotypes

According to the Centers for Disease Control, and Department of Health and Human Services, it is your children, and not those of the urban ghetto, who are most likely to use drugs. That's right: white high school students are seven times more likely than blacks to have used cocaine; eight times more likely to have smoked crack; ten times more likely to have used LSD and seven times more likely to have used heroin. In fact, there are more white high school students who have used crystal methamphetamine (the most addictive drug on the streets) than there are black students who smoke cigarettes.

What's more, white youth ages 12–17 are more likely to sell drugs: 34% more likely, in fact than their black counterparts. And it is white youth who are twice as likely to binge drink, and nearly twice as likely as blacks to drive drunk. And white males are twice as likely to bring a weapon to school as are black males.

And yet I would bet a valued body part that there aren't 100 white people in Santee, California, or most any other "nice" community who have ever heard a single one of the statistics above. Even though they were collected by government agencies using these folks' tax money for the purpose. Because the media doesn't report on white dysfunction.

A few years ago, *U.S. News* ran a story entitled: "A Shocking Look at Blacks and Crime." Yet never have they or any other news outlet discussed the "shocking" whiteness of these shoot-em-ups. Indeed, every time media commentators discuss the similarities in these crimes they mention that the shooters were boys, they were loners, they got picked on, but never do they seem to notice a certain highly visible melanin deficiency. Color-blind, I guess.

White-blind is more like it, as I figure these folks would spot color mighty damn quick were some of it to stroll into their community. Santee's whiteness is so taken for granted by its residents that the Mayor, in that CNN interview, thought nothing of saying on the one hand that the town was 82 percent white, but on the other hand that "this is America." Well that isn't America, and it especially isn't California, where whites are only half of the population. This is a town that is removed from America, and yet its Mayor thinks they are the normal ones—so much so that when asked about racial diversity, he replied that there weren't many of different "ethni-tis-tities." Not a word. Not even close.

I'd like to think that after this one, people would wake up. Take note. Rethink their stereotypes of who the dangerous ones are. But deep down, I know better. The folks hitting the snooze button on this none-too-subtle alarm are my own people, after all, and I know their blindness like the back of my hand.

8

The Absence of Public Morality Causes School Shootings

Jude P. Dougherty

Jude P. Dougherty is a dean emeritus and professor of philosophy at the Catholic University of America in Washington, D.C.

School shootings suggest that society has failed to teach its members a publicly accepted system of morality. Although the perpetrators of the school shootings at Littleton and other campuses have been surrounded by dangerous influences, such as television and the Internet, to which they do not know how to respond, they are responsible for their own behavior. The way to improve society is to improve individuals. Society, in particular parents, must take steps to ensure that children know the difference between right and wrong.

The lawyer who persuaded the Columbine family to sue the parents of the Littleton, Colorado, killers may not be guilty of malpractice, but he is seriously lacking in his understanding of human nature. No force, parental, school, or media, compelled the shootings. Far from being coerced, the killings were planned by rational human beings who knew what they were doing. Failure to acknowledge this fact reduces the killers to the animal level on a par with Pavlov's dogs responding to stimuli. "To blame the fault of a creature is to praise its essential nature," says Augustine in his treatise, *On Free Choice of the Will.*

Personal responsibility

Granted that the killers were influenced by their environment, but other students subjected to the same or a similar environment have not perpetrated a comparable deed. Those concerned need to face it: The killers were solely responsible for their own conduct. Suing their parents doesn't make any more sense than suing the writers of the textbooks used in the

Reprinted, with permission, from "Assessing Blame," by Jude P. Dougherty, *The Wanderer*, August 26, 1999.

classroom or the judges and courts that have effectively taken moral teaching out of the common school. Recognizing this does not suggest that the content of those textbooks and the philosophical attitudes of the teachers are unimportant. Ultimately what the student makes of the sources available to him and to the stimuli surrounding him in and out of school is up to him. Students, like the rest of the population, determine their own mode of life. There is no psychologically determining factor that forces the evil deed or, for that matter, the generous act.

This is not to deny that the young are influenced by their surroundings. Just the opposite; young minds are especially vulnerable. Wise parents are careful to monitor the literature to which their children have access and even more so the movies and television shows they are likely to watch, and now the Internet. Parents in every generation warn against bad companions and morally precarious situations, yet no cautionary admonition or parental monitoring can forge the perfect youth. The youngster remains responsible for yielding to the influence.

It behooves us to attend to the beliefs to which impressionable youth are exposed.

Responsible parents nevertheless attempt to train for the better, respecting the age and development of the child. Very young children are taught to say "please" and "thank you," to "think of others first," to say their prayers, to wipe their feet before entering the house, to wash their hands before meals. This teaching is often accompanied by discipline, sometimes corporal. The intent is to establish habits that will serve well not only in childhood but throughout life. The child who does not experience such instruction and discipline is deprived, but is not without intelligence. It doesn't take much intelligence or experience to recognize that certain modes of behavior are inappropriate or have disastrous consequences. Absent a stern father, one can still know the difference between the rights and wrongs of daily life.

The philosopher Immanuel Kant wrote, "There is nothing more fundamental than a good will." Kant speaks of a "virtuous disposition." The presence or absence of good will can be detected in very young children. The capacity for doing or refraining from doing is the capacity for choice, free will if you like. Appropriate training or its absence does not deprive one of choice for good or for ill. Good parents and good teachers will inspire the intelligent and well disposed, but not inevitably. The child, the student, remains free to reject even the loftiest examples. The bad apple in the crowd is a metaphor founded on reality. Children influence each other for good and for ill. That said, we need to attend to those things that promote virtue.

William Bennett attempted to do this in his *Book of Virtues*, a collation of texts designed to promote virtue by fostering "right opinion." When published, it quickly became a best-seller. Through a collection of appropriate writings, some ancient, some contemporary, Bennett sought to provide easy access to timeless teaching about human nature and personal responsibility.

Destroying or improving society

We read of campaigns of vandalism and arson perpetrated on businesses in a small West Coast city by black-hooded youths, who smashed windows and dumped stolen merchandise into a nearby fountain. Newspaper columnists may refer to them as disaffected youth, but that term masks something sinister. The young anarchists were apparently inspired by the words of a middle-aged writer whose books and essays teach that humanity's best hope lies in "smashing civilization back to the level of hunters and gatherers." Those culpable of the vandalism were said to believe, as taught by their mentor, that trashing the property of corporations and the state is righteous, given the harm those institutions have inflicted on the earth.

While it does not take much intelligence to know that killing others or destroying their property or good name is wrong, it may take greater intelligence and some training to see through the sophistical arguments or ideology that can inspire such activity. Rhetoric is an ancient art that can be used for good or ill, to inspire noble or demonic activity. The innocent or unreflective can be swayed by voice and even more by an image. It is not without reason that we say a picture is worth a thousand words. Battle flags, drums, rousing speeches are the instruments of encouragement from political rallies to the battlefield. The mob aroused can be commanded. Enter the role of critical intelligence, lauded by generations of professional educators. But the "critical intelligence" taught in the American common school has been directed at the very things that have created Western civilization and the rule of law that we inherited.

Because the moral character of a society begins with the individual, society can never be greater or better than the individuals who constitute it. The way to improve society is to improve individuals. This involves the encouragement of self-control and restraint, both classical virtues which receive little support from contemporary liberals.

As Edmund Burke wrote in 1791, "Men are qualified for civil liberty in exact proportion to their disposition to put moral chains upon their own appetites . . . society cannot exist unless a controlling power upon will and appetite be placed somewhere, and the less of it there is within, the more there is without. It is ordained in the eternal constitution of things that men of intemperate minds cannot be free. Their passions forge their fetters."

Re-examining modern culture

To arrive at the true causality of the crime, one has to make a number of important distinctions, beginning with the acknowledgment of a difference among the cause, the condition, and the occasion of a deed. In the execution of any deed or the production of any artifact, it is necessary to distinguish further among the causal elements at play. The ancients distinguished among the craftsmen, his purpose, the matter with which he worked, and the structure he wished to impose, a fourfold distinction.

Clearly the Littleton killers executed the deed in the light of a purpose. That purpose needs examining. At one level it is all too evident, i.e., creating fear in the student body and the subsequent killing of students whose ill fortune was to be nearby. The summary killing of the young woman who professed to believe in God may or may not have been planned. Either way, it tells us something about the attitude of the killers. Needless to say, it is not normal for young people to go about killing. What then inspired the deed? To talk about "disaffected youth," "warped minds" doesn't explain but points in the right direction. Before the deed, there is the thought. It can augur for good or for evil. St. Paul lamented, "The good I would, I do not." Good intentions as well as bad intentions can lead to action, but neither compels one to action. We live in the light of a set of ideas. Some are beliefs about what is the case; some are ideals about what ought to be. With respect to the latter, if I subscribe to the Mosaic Code, I am more likely to keep holy the Sabbath and to honor my parents than if I do not. I may believe that downtown merchants exploit the poor, but the license to destroy or steal their property requires yet a different belief. I may believe that animals ought not be killed for their fur, but throwing paint on someone's mink coat requires subscription to another set of beliefs. Karl Marx may sanction violence; St. Francis de Sales, never.

The Littleton tragedy points clearly to the need to re-examine the sources of our culture.

It behooves us to attend to the beliefs to which impressionable youth are exposed, not only beliefs about matters of fact but those beliefs that provide purpose or meaning to life. If I do not believe in God or a natural order to which I am accountable, I am without a rudder. Sense appetite, untempered by rational consideration, is not a sure guide. No one can for long remain without beliefs concerning the conduct of life. Most inherit through the family a moral outlook, usually rooted in religious belief. We speak of Western culture, distinguishing it from Islamic and Eastern cultures. That culture, in spite of attempts to suppress its origins, is Christian at its core. For ideological reasons, the common school has suppressed the religious source of the values we hold dear, without replacing it with any clear alternative.

Admittedly, religion is not the only source of morality. Lofty moral teaching is present in Aristotle and in the Stoics. Classical philosophy is certainly to be valued as a moral source, but its effectiveness as a tutor is slight compared with that provided by biblical religion. The issue that needs to be addressed is how to surmount the secular activism that has influenced the courts and determined social policy at variance with the U.S. constitutional protection of the free exercise of religion. Can a society, indeed a culture, survive if everything is permitted? The vast majority of today's citizens have no inkling as to what or to whom they owe their liberty and prosperity. They are unaware of what a debilitating effect the destruction of the nation's moral compass will have on their lives in the long run.

The Littleton tragedy points clearly to the need to re-examine the sources of our culture and the rule of law it supports. The lack of a publicly accepted, coherent system of morality is one of the great misfortunes of our age.

9

The Immaturity of the Adolescent Brain Can Lead to School Shootings

Daniel R. Weinberger

Daniel R. Weinberger is the chief of the Clinical Brain Disorders Branch, Division of Intramural Research Programs, at the National Institute of Mental Health.

School shootings occur because the prefrontal cortex in a teenage brain is not fully developed. The prefrontal cortex is the part of the brain that enables people to act rationally and resist violent impulses. However, the cortex is not fully functional until at least two decades after birth. Consequently, the adolescents responsible for school shootings are unable to control their impulses and are unaware of the long-range consequences of their actions.

[M]arch 2001's] shootings at Santana High School in California led quickly to now-familiar attempts to explain the seemingly unexplainable in terms of culture and circumstance: violent entertainment, a lack of accountability for deviant behavior, broken homes. While each of these issues may play some role in the tragedies of school shootings, to understand what goes wrong in the teenagers who fire the guns, you have to understand something about the biology of the teenage brain.

Controlling violent impulses

Andy Williams, the boy held in the Santana shootings, is 15. Many other school shooters have been about the same age or even younger. And the brain of a 15-year-old is not mature—particularly in an area called the prefrontal cortex, which is critical to good judgment and the suppression of impulse.

The human brain has required many millennia and many evolutionary stages to reach its current complex status. It enables us to do all kinds of amazing and uniquely human things: to unravel the human genome, to imagine the future, to fall in love. As part of its capacity for achievement, it must also be able to exercise control that stops maladaptive behavior. Everyone gets angry; everybody has felt a desire for vengeance. The capacity to control impulses that arise from these feelings is a function of the prefrontal cortex.

This is the part that distinguishes our brain most decisively from those of all other animals, even our closest relatives. It allows us to act on the basis of reason. It can preclude an overwhelming tendency for action, (e.g., to run from a fire in a crowded theater), because an abstract memory (e.g., "don't panic,") makes more sense. It knows that all that glitters is not gold. Without a prefrontal cortex, it would be impossible to have societies based on moral and legal codes.

The 15-year-old brain does not have the biological machinery to inhibit impulses in the service of long-range planning.

Sometimes violent behavior may be adaptive (for example, in self-defense), in which case the prefrontal cortex will help plan an effective strategy. However, controlling violent impulses when they are maladaptive can be a very taxing duty for the prefrontal cortex, especially if the desire for action is great or if the brain is weakened in its capacity to exercise such control.

Many factors can impair the capacity of the prefrontal cortex to serve its full impulse-control function: for example, neurological diseases that kill cells in the prefrontal cortex, head injuries that damage these cells, alcohol and drugs that impair their function, and biological immaturity.

The thought process of the adolescent brain

The inhibitory functions are not present at birth; it takes many years for the necessary biological processes to hone a prefrontal cortex into an effective, efficient executive. These processes are now being identified by scientific research. They involve how nerve cells communicate with each other, how they form interactive networks to handle complex computational tasks and how they respond to experience. It takes at least two decades to form a fully functional prefrontal cortex.

Scientists have shown that the pace of the biological refinements quickens considerably in late adolescence, as the brain makes a final maturational push to tackle the exigencies of independent adult life. But the evidence is unequivocal that the prefrontal cortex of a 15-year-old is biologically immature. The connections are not final, the networks are still being strengthened and the full capacity for inhibitory control is still years away.

The 15-year-old brain does not have the biological machinery to inhibit impulses in the service of long-range planning. This is why it is important for adults to help children make plans and set rules, and why institutions are created to impose limits on behavior that children are incapable of limiting. Parents provide their children with a lend-lease prefrontal cortex during all those years that it takes to grow one, particularly when the inner urges for impulsive action intensify.

Adolescents have always had to deal with feeling hurt, ashamed and powerless. In the face of ridicule, they may want revenge. Thirty years ago, a teenager in this position might have started a fight, maybe even pulled a knife. If he was afraid that he could not defend himself, he might have recruited a tough guy to help him out. One way or another, he would have tried to teach his tormentors a lesson. Very likely, however, no one would have died.

But times have changed, and now this angry teenager lives in a culture that romanticizes gunplay, and he may well have access to guns. I doubt that most school shooters intend to kill, in the adult sense of permanently ending a life and paying the price for the rest of their own lives. Such intention would require a fully developed prefrontal cortex, which could anticipate the future and rationally appreciate cause and effect. The young school shooter probably does not think about the specifics of shooting at all. The often reported lack of apparent remorse illustrates how unreal the reality is to these teenagers.

This brief lesson in brain development is not meant to absolve criminal behavior or make the horrors any less unconscionable. But the shooter at Santana High, like other adolescents, needed people or institutions to prevent him from being in a potentially deadly situation where his immature brain was left to its own devices. No matter what the town or the school, if a gun is put in the control of the prefrontal cortex of a hurt and vengeful 15-year-old, and it is pointed at a human target, it will very likely go off.

10

Schools Can Take Steps to Reduce School Shootings

Jonathan Lane

Jonathan Lane is the principal of Warden Middle School in Warden, Washington.

It is the responsibility of schools to implement policies that will reduce the occurrence of school shootings. These policies can include zero tolerance policies (automatic suspension or expulsion when a student brings a weapon to school), values education, classes on conflict resolution, and counseling services. However, the community as a whole must play a part in preventing violence. For example, the entertainment industry needs to deemphasize violence in its movies, video games, and music.

M r. Chairman, distinguished members of the Committee. My name is Jonathan Lane. I am here today representing myself and the National Association of Secondary School Principals (NASSP). I am currently the Principal of Warden Middle School in Warden, Washington, but the reason I am here is because of a tragic event that occurred in February of 1996 at Frontier Jr. High School in Moses Lake, Washington.

I have always said that I would take any opportunity to try to make something positive out of this terrible tragedy. I have been reminded again recently by the shootings in Colorado how such a senseless act can impact a community and even the whole country. The reasons that these shootings have taken place are varied and complex. Solutions are not easily found and will require communities working together to solve fundamental problems that affect our whole society.

A firsthand experience

Let me tell you my story. It was February 2, 1996. I was teaching down the hall when I heard something unusual. I didn't know what the sound was but I knew that it wasn't right. I went down the hall and opened the door and discovered students in a state of terror—some sitting at desks,

From Jonathan Lane's testimony before the U.S. House of Representatives, Committee on Education and the Workforce, Subcommittee on Early Childhood, Youth, and Families, May 18, 1999.

and others sitting or lying on the floor. As soon as I smelled gunsmoke, I realized what had happened and I dove for the floor and hid behind the teacher's desk.

As I lay on the floor behind the desk I discovered the teacher, Mrs. Caires, lying right next to me against the chalkboard. She had died instantly and still held the eraser and white board marker in her hand. I saw the students in various states of shock and the look of terror and death on their faces, and wondered if I was going to be next. Barry, the student who had fired the shots, was standing in the corner of the classroom, dressed head to toe in black—black trenchcoat, black cowboy boots, black jeans, and a black cowboy hat. He wore a gunbelt and had two handguns, 83 rounds of ammunition, and a white lucky rabbit's foot hanging from his belt.

Barry called me by name and told me to stand up, but I told him I couldn't. I was too afraid. I wouldn't stand up until he said that if I did not, he was going to start shooting more kids. I knew I had to make the situation better. I stood up when Barry assured me that he was not going to hurt anyone else. Through negotiation, and with the help of other students, I was able to get two injured students and a student with diabetes out of the room.

A variety of measures must be put in place if we are to effectively address school safety concerns.

Barry later told me that I was going to be a hostage. He was going to put the gun in my mouth and we were going to leave the room. Again, I told him that I couldn't, and that I was too afraid. I was five or six feet from Barry, and knew that it was my best opportunity to end the situation. I charged him and pinned him against the wall with my body, grabbing his hands on the stock of the gun. At that time, the police came in and the kids went out. I guess it was quite a sight, but I was focusing on not letting him go until the police had him on the ground.

I have thought a lot about the incident and have come to some conclusions about how I acted and why I was able to help end the situation without further harm. I have always been a wrestler. I believe that this training helped me to keep my composure and function in a stressful situation. Those many hours I spent in the wrestling room and on the mats during competition were a preparation for this situation. I believe that healthy competition through sports prepares all of us for life's challenges.

Teachers are not taught what to do during a hostage situation in Education 101 and I don't think I, in my wildest dream, ever thought that sometime during my teaching career I would experience a gun in a classroom. I believe that ordinary people who make good choices in their lives are able to do extraordinary things when placed in a terrible situation. Individuals learn how to make these choices through their peers and the example of others.

We all make choices in our lives. There are big choices and there are small choices. Good small choices add up to good big results when it counts. This holds true for children and youth as well as adults. I believe that Barry made many choices in his life that resulted in a terrible incident that has affected many people's lives. Barry chose to surround himself with violent movies and books. He chose to deal with his problems in a negative manner. He was unable or incapable of making good choices.

We need to recognize when someone is in trouble and need to find those who can help. This is especially true for students. Help may be a friend, a family member, a counselor, or a minister; it may be a teacher, a policeman, or a professional health care worker. I believe that additional counselors are another important piece in helping prevent similar tragedies from happening in the future.

Handguns and semi-automatic weapons must be kept out of schools.

When I was in the classroom I was afraid. I believe I used my fear in a positive way to help me deal with the situation. We cannot let fear prevent us from making the right choices. Fear can be an obstacle or a motivation. Fear can paralyze us or it can be used in a positive manner to help us overcome adversity. I knew that when I was in that classroom I was the teacher and it was my responsibility to try to make it better. I believe that teachers are heroes every time they walk into a classroom and try to better their students' lives. Teachers and principals deserve all the respect and gratitude that we can give them.

My heroes are my parents, teachers, and coaches. Bob Mason, my wrestling coach, my teacher, and my friend, is certainly one of my heroes. We all need to choose heroes in our lives that exemplify positive. Choose your heroes well and try to do those things that make your community a better place to live.

Ways to improve school safety

Shortly after the shooting, the community of Moses Lake formed a "Blue Ribbon task force" that looked at the community as a whole and tried to come up with some positive approaches to help solve some of the problems that face young people. The committee looked at everything from violence in the theaters, television and video rental stores, to lack of out of school activities for young people, the use of school uniforms, and coordination of services to help families in need. There was broad-based participation from all factions of the community and there were many recommendations made.

Some things that were implemented were support of an organization called "Youth Partnership Task Force," organization of a Boys and Girls Club, and use of school uniforms at the middle school level. The community as a whole tried to work together to address the problems facing young people. We have adopted a program called "Virtuous Reality" that promotes positive character values throughout our community.

High schools and middle schools have developed crisis plans, hired security officers, reviewed discipline policies, adopted no tolerance policies concerning violence, installed surveillance cameras, and increased security overall. The greatest change is that everyone is more sensitive to the fact that we all need to work together to meet the needs of our young people. There isn't just one answer or one program that will "fix" the problems. It requires involvement of students, parents, teachers, churches and many other community groups. Moses Lake is making progress but we all have a long way to go.

Indeed, a variety of measures must be put in place if we are to effectively address school safety concerns.

- A zero tolerance policy must be taken concerning weapons in schools, and gun laws need to be enforced and strengthened.
- Communities and schools must advocate and model to students a set of core values.
- Schools must personalize the education of each child.
- Policies and procedures for addressing violent incidents on campus need to be put in place at each school.
- Counseling and mentoring services need to be available to all children.
- The media and entertainment industry need to accept their responsibility in curbing the portrayal of violent acts as a form of entertainment.
- Peer mediation training should be included in teacher preparation courses.
- Parents should be trained in violence prevention strategies that emphasize easy access to handguns and other weapons.

"Youngsters who are intimidated and fearful cannot be at ease; they cannot give education the single-minded attention needed for success." This statement appears in the school reform publication *Breaking Ranks: Changing an American Institution* produced by NASSP and the Carnegie Foundation for the Advancement of Teaching. One of the key messages provided in this seminal document is that schools must be safe and effective environments conducive to teaching and learning if our students are to prosper.

The community as a whole must make our children and school safety a priority.

In order for these environments to exist, handguns and semi-automatic weapons must be kept out of schools and out of the hands of those who abuse their use. A major 1993 Louis Harris poll about guns among American youth reports that 1 in 25 students have taken a handgun to school in a single month, and 59 percent know where to get a handgun if they need one. NASSP supported passage of the Brady Act and the Gun Free Schools Act and continues to support laws which restrict the sale of these weapons and that require all handguns to have a child safety lock. Even though these laws could not prevent all violence in schools, they would help forestall the deadly level of violence these weapons were designed to create from being readily available for use in our schools by and against our children.

Principals need training on how to identify and implement strategies to make each school safer. NASSP has made this a priority and is seeking funding to subsidize the training of instructors who will work with principals in every state to make their schools safer. Additional training for principals, teachers, and parents needs to focus on student behavior and the identification of students "at risk" of becoming violent or in need of assistance before tragedies occur. Conflict resolution skills need to be included in teacher preparation courses and in the general curriculum of all elementary and secondary schools in this country.

Teaching a core set of values

Equally important to the preventative measures mentioned above is instilling students with a core set of values. The students who committed the horrific acts at Columbine, West Paducah, and Pearl, lacked a core set of values. At Frontier Jr. High, it was believed the shooting was motivated by students harassing and picking on the shooter. Principals, teachers, parents, and the community as a whole, need to teach students about such key virtues as honesty, dependability, trust, responsibility, tolerance, and respect.

Many middle schools and high schools have become large and impersonal, causing those students who feel disconnected from their peers, their school, and their community to feel further isolated. Something needs to be done to make the educational environment more personal for each student. Recommendations for personalizing the educational environment contained in *Breaking Ranks* include limiting the size of schools to no more than 600 students, the creation of schools within schools to meet the 600 student limit, the creation of an adult advocate for each student, and a personalized educational plan for each student.

Youth need to be taught how to deal with feelings of anger and aggression in constructive and non-violent ways, and be provided with outlets for that energy. Not only does this include the more visible acts of violence, but also smaller infractions such as teasing, bullying, verbal abuse, and harassment. Sports and co-curricular activities are an important and necessary part of the educational process that provide venues for this type of instruction. After-school programs are also supplying many youth with productive options as opposed to unsupervised "free time" which has led to trouble for many youth.

NASSP has partnered with *Community of Caring,* a project of the Joseph P. Kennedy, Jr. Foundation, to aid with values education. Through teacher training, values discussion, student forums, family involvement, and community service, students are shunning violence, gaining feelings of self-worth, and making positive decisions about their future. Other service organizations such as *Community of Caring* are committed to the task of providing students alternatives to violent behavior and bleak futures.

Students need to be invested with the sense that their actions and lives do make a difference. Several organizations including NASSP, the National Association of Student Councils, the United Way of America, the National PTA, the Council of Great City Schools, the American Federation of Teachers, and the National Education Association have encouraged students to sign a pledge against gun violence. Activities such as these are building blocks that set a "values" foundation for many students.

Linking schools and community

Principals, teachers, and schools alone will not be able to prevent violence. The community as a whole must make our children and school safety a priority. Parents, friends, and citizens in general, must remember they are role models setting examples for children. Those who own guns should act responsibly, keeping these weapons under lock and key and out of the hands of youth. Parental involvement programs should include training for parents in violence prevention strategies that emphasize the dangers of easy access to handguns and other weapons.

And the word "community" means the greater community. NASSP has urged the broadcasting and motion picture industries to work with educators and parents in moving toward a significant reduction of violent acts in television and film programming. An average American child will have witnessed hundreds of thousands of acts of violence upon graduation from high school. This proliferation of violent images desensitizes children to violence and the finality of violent acts. The entertainment industry must step forward and accept their responsibility in reducing the number of violent portrayals in film, music, video games, and on the Internet. No one else can make this happen today so that our children can have a better less violent future.

Congress has implemented several programs that have assisted principals, teachers, and communities address school safety, the NASSP supports the continuation of programs such as the Community Oriented Policing Services (COPS) program, and the Safe and Drug Free Schools and Communities program. In addition, the Safe Schools/Healthy Students Initiative (SSHTI) announced by the President [in 1999] provides an excellent community-wide approach to solving schools' safety needs; and the proposed School Emergency Response to Violence (SERV) project will institute for schools a necessary FEMA-like plan in the unfortunate event that another violent incident occurs.

In conclusion, there is not just one answer but multiple strategies that are needed to address the issue of school safety. Prevention is the key, whether it be in the form of limiting access to weapons, securing facilities, instilling core values, training school personnel and parents, limiting violent images, or identifying early the students "at risk" of performing violent acts. Each school must find the right mix of prevention activities and must be diligent in continuing to assess the atmosphere on campus. School safety and the value of our children need to be made a priority by our principals, teachers, students, communities and government in order for us to prevent future catastrophes.

Thank you Mr. Chairman. I would be happy to take any questions you or the Committee may have.

11

Schools Are Taking Unnecessary Steps to Reduce School Shootings

Michael Easterbrook

Michael Easterbrook is a freelance writer and regular contributor to the online health magazine HealthScout.

Some of the steps taken by schools to prevent school shootings—for example, metal detectors, security guards, and punishment of students who use violent language—have had ill effects. Schools punish students who use violent language without considering the context of those statements or the behavioral history of the students. Increased security can create a sense of helplessness that makes adolescents feel like prisoners and increases their fascination with violent resistance. Instead of relying on punishments that alienate their students, schools should provide a nurturing environment and increased access to counseling.

Tension in the classroom had been building all year. The English teacher was fresh out of college and her pupils, about 15 of them, were seniors on the advanced-placement track at South Fayette High School outside of Pittsburgh, Pennsylvania. These stellar students weren't accustomed to pulling grades below an A, but the teacher was infuriatingly tough, frequently returning papers marked C and D. "It was kind of like a little war," says Matt Welch, the class president and one of the students. "It just seemed like she was out to get us."

A growing sensitivity to violent language

If there was one person the teacher really seemed to have it in for, it was Aaron Leese. A bold 18-year-old with short red hair, Leese was popular with his classmates, if not exactly your model student. Police had busted him in the park with a bottle of bourbon. In school, he had a habit of embarrassing the teacher by asking her questions in front of the class that she found hard to answer. Leese also didn't take kindly to low marks on his assignments. Once, he was so riled by a grade that the teacher asked him to leave. As he was walking out he muttered something like "troglodyte bitch," which earned him a three-day suspension.

The relationship between the two became increasingly strained. One morning in spring, she handed back one of the year's last big assignments, a 10-page essay on a book of one's choice. Leese had written his on Thomas Moore's *Utopia*. He needed an A to pass the class, but he received a D. "I said, 'Man, if I don't pass this class, I'm going to be mad enough to kill,'" Leese recalls. "It was something I said out of frustration. After that the teacher said, 'That could be misinterpreted, you know?' I said, 'Yeah, my bad. I take it back.'"

The exchange went so quickly that a student who sat directly behind Leese didn't even catch it. But it made a distinct impression on the teacher. After class ended, she reported it to the principal, who pulled Leese into his office and phoned the police. By noon, Leese was being escorted off school grounds by two officers from the South Fayette Township Police Department. He was now facing criminal charges. "I was in tears," Leese says.

Had Leese made his comment just five years ago instead of in spring 1998, it might well have gone unnoticed. But a string of deadly shootings at schools around the country is radically altering how these institutions interact with their students. Since February 1996, the massacres, seven in all, have left a total of 35 students, teachers and principals dead. In the latest tragedy at Columbine High School in Littleton, Colorado, two youths killed 13 before taking their own lives.

Alarmed by such incidents, educators are changing the way they go about their mission—and the steps some are taking go far beyond a heightened sensitivity to violent language. They're installing spiked fences, metal detectors, emergency alert systems. They're hiring security guards and imposing searches of students' bags, lockers and desks. And they're insisting that teachers learn skills not included in any syllabus: how to run lockdown drills, how to strip a student vigilante of his weapon.

Overreacting to language

No one would deny that educators have a right—make that an obligation—to do all they can to protect themselves and their charges from what has become a prime threat to their safety: students themselves. But worrisome questions have arisen about the effects such measures are having on the education which is the schools' purpose to provide. More disturbing still are suggestions that the efforts may not be effectively preventing trouble—and may even be promoting it.

The change most immediately apparent to students has been the move to punish those who use violent language. It's hard to fault administrators for paying close attention to such outbursts. Reporters delving into the lives of the young killers invariably have surfaced with tales of suspicious remarks made before the carnage. Like Barry Loukaitis, the 14-year-old who killed two students and a teacher at Frontier Middle School in Moses Lake, Washington, who told a friend how cool it would be to go on a shooting spree. Or Kip Kinkel, accused of killing four people at

Thurston High School in Springfield, Oregon, who talked frequently of shooting cats, blowing up cows and building bombs. And more recently still, Eric Harris, one of the Columbine shooters, who posted a message on the Internet saying, "You all better hide in your houses because I'm coming for everyone, and I will shoot to kill and I will kill everyone." Remarks like these, recalled with remorse after the fact, have led principals and teachers to be on the lookout for more of the same. But when do such comments represent an actual intent to kill, and when are they merely the product of an active fantasy life?

Robby Stango, for example, was a 15-year-old freshman at Kingston High School in upstate New York in May 1998 when school officials were alerted to a poem he had written for a class assignment. Titled "Step to Oblivion," the poem is about a divorced man who decides one night to jump off a cliff and end his life. "Here I am/Standing here on this gloomy night/Minutes away from my horrid fate," the verse begins. The precipice is only seven feet high, however, and the man survives the fall. "Maybe my prayer was answered/Or it could have been just luck/But I was given a second chance at life," the poem concludes.

Despite its positive ending, the verse convinced school officials that Stango was headed for trouble. Although the teen was seeing a counselor at the time about problems he was having at home, he didn't pose a danger to himself or others, according to therapists familiar with his case. Yet the school's discovery of the poem set off a chain of events that resulted in Stango being forced, against his mother's wishes, into a five-night stay in a psychiatric ward. Alice Stango has since filed a lawsuit against the school district and the county.

Worrisome questions have arisen about the effects [safety] measures are having on . . . education.

It was also writing assignments for English class that got eighth-grader Troy Foley, from the California coastal town of Half Moon Bay, in trouble. In an essay titled "The Riot," Foley, then 14, wrote of a kid who is so enraged with school rules, especially the ones forbidding him to wear a hat and drink soda during class, that he incites a student riot that ends with the principal getting bludgeoned to death. Two weeks later, Foley handed in "Goin' Postal," an equally violent tale about a character named Martin who sneaks a pistol into school and kills a police officer, the vice principal and principal. Though he had no history of violent or even disruptive behavior, Foley was suspended for five days for making a terroristic threat. Foley's mother, assisted by the American Civil Liberties Union, managed to have the record changed to state that Foley was suspended for two days for using profanity in school assignments. Foley has since skipped high school and is enrolled at a two-year community college.

Parents and lawyers of both boys contend that the schools overreacted in these cases, punishing children whose only crime was a vivid imagination. But even if that's so, it leaves an important question unanswered: how do principals and teachers know when a violent story or remark signals a real threat? Those who turn to psychological research will find only equivocal answers at best.

"These things may be indicators, and they may not," says Kevin Dwyer, Ph.D., president-elect of the National Association of School Psychologists. "To try to predict an individual's future behavior based on what they say or write isn't really possible." His view is shared by Edward Taylor, Ph.D., professor of social work at the University of Illinois at Urbana-Champaign and an expert on childhood mental illness. "I don't know of any study that has empirically examined whether the use of violent language in creative writing can actually predict those who are going to commit a crime," declares Taylor. Such language so permeates American popular culture, he notes, that its use doesn't necessarily indicate a predilection for the use of force.

Schools have increased security

Mindful of the complexities involved in predicting which students will become violent, many school districts are attempting to circumvent the threat entirely by altering their physical landscapes. Located in the small town of West Paducah, Kentucky, on the banks of the Ohio River, Heath High School was dragged into the national spotlight in the winter of 1997 when 14-year-old Michael Carneal gunned down classmates, killing three girls. The school quickly convened a security committee, which authorized a $148,000 security plan.

Today, Heath requires visitors, teachers and students to wear identification tags around their necks at all times, like soldiers. It has students sign consent forms authorizing staff to rummage through backpacks and cars for weapons; each morning before entering school, students line up to have their bags searched. Heath also has hired a uniformed, armed security guard. Officials have prepared should a weapon slip by security. They've purchased two-way radios for staff members to wear on their belts, in case they need to communicate during an attack. And they've placed emergency medical kits and disaster-instruction manuals in each classroom.

Surrounding troubled young people with the accoutrements of a police state may only fuel their fascination with guns.

The new environment at Heath High School dismays many parents and students. "They made my son sign papers so they can search his possessions, his locker, anything, anytime," says one unhappy parent. "From what I understand, the Constitution is still in effect. I don't like the idea of my child going to school and having school officials search him at their discretion. They're trying their best, but they don't seem to be getting it right."

Heath's principal Bill Bond defends the measures. "We have restrictions on everything we do," he points out. "I've never thought about carrying a bomb on an airplane, but I pass through airport security just like everybody else. The very concept of security is always going to reduce freedom. That is a trade-off people have been dealing with since the beginning of time."

Schools around the country are following Heath's lead. In April 1998, an Indiana school district became the first in the country to install metal detectors in its elementary schools, after three of its students were caught bringing guns into the buildings. [In January 1999], the U.S. Department of Education reported that nearly 6300 students were expelled in the 1996–1997 school year for carrying firearms: 58% had handguns, 7% rifles or shotguns and 35% other weapons, including bombs and grenades. Faced with such statistics, more schools than ever before are buying security devices like spiked fences, motorized gates and blast-proof metal covers for doors and windows. Administrators are also signing up in droves for the services of security experts. Jesus Villahermosa Jr., a deputy sheriff in Pierce County, Washington, expects to run 65 sessions for educators this year, double the number held in 1997. "I'm completely booked," says Villahermosa, whose curriculum includes how to disarm students and how to run lock-down drills.

Such measures may make schools feel less vulnerable, but how do they affect the learning that goes on inside? Here again, research provides only tentative answers. Citing neurological and psychological research, Renate Nummela Caine, professor emeritus of educational psychology at California State University-San Bernadino, maintains that when students feel threatened or helpless, their brains "downshift" into more primitive states, and their ability to think becomes automatic and limited, instinctive rather than creative.

Regimented classrooms, inflexible teachers, an atmosphere of suspicion, can all induce feelings of helplessness, contends Caine, author with her husband Geoffrey Caine, a law professor turned educational specialist, of *Making Connections: Teaching and the Human Brain* (Addison-Wesley, 1994). "What schools are doing is creating conditions that are comparable to prisons," she declares. "Where else are people searched every day and watched every minute? They want to clamp down and they want control. It's based on fear, and it's an understandable reaction given the circumstances, but the problem is that they're not looking at other solutions."

The ill effects of punishments

Psychologists say that surrounding troubled young people with the accoutrements of a police state may only fuel their fascination with guns and increase their resistance to authority. Likewise, punishing young people for talking or writing about their violent musings may just force the fantasies underground, where they may grow more exaggerated and extreme. "It's a response that says, 'We don't know how to react, so we're going to respond harshly,'" says Patrick Tolan, Ph.D., professor of adolescent development and intervention at the University of Illinois-Chicago. "If you're a child, would you come forward and say you're troubled in that atmosphere? Are you going to rely on adults if that is how simplistically they think about things? Rather than saying something to a counselor, you might well keep quiet."

Suspending or expelling a student, moreover, strips him of the structure of school and the company of people he knows, perhaps deepening his alienation and driving him to more desperate acts. Kip Kinkel, for example, went on his rampage after being suspended from school for possessing a stolen handgun.

Yet there are punishments more severe and alienating than suspensions and expulsions. As schools begin to resemble police precincts, school officials are abdicating their duty to counsel and discipline unruly students and letting the cops down the hall handle the classroom disruptions, bullying and schoolyard fights. And the cops aren't taking any chances. They're arresting students and feeding them into a criminal justice system that sees little distinction between kids and adults. "Once that police officer is on the scene, the principals and teachers lose control completely," says Vincent Shiraldi, executive director of the Justice Policy Institute in Washington. "I think it will make students a more litigious group and much less able to solve their problems peacefully and reasonably."

Taking a different approach to school safety

There may be a better way, and educators are beginning to look for it. Instead of building schools like fortresses, architects are experimenting with ways to open them up and make them more welcoming. Designers are lowering lockers to waist-height and in some cases eliminating them entirely, so students can't hide behind them or use them as storage spaces for guns. Instead of being built on the outskirts of a school, administrative offices are being placed in the middle, enclosed in glass walls so officials can see what's going on. Gymnasiums and auditoriums are being opened to the public, serving as meeting places for the local chamber of commerce or performing arts group. "The kids feel nurtured by this," says Steven Bingler, a school architect in New Orleans who participated [in October 1998] in a symposium on making schools safer that was sponsored by the U.S. Department of Education and the White House Millennium Council. "School doesn't feel like a prison to them anymore."

On a more personal level, some schools are offering increased access to counselors; others have hired a "violence prevention coordinator" to whom students can give anonymous tips about classmates in trouble. In accord with this less punitive, more therapeutic approach, students who use threatening language are being steered into anger-management programs, intensive therapy and to other support services.

As for Aaron Leese, he was charged with making a terroristic threat and thrown in a holding cell for the afternoon. "My thought was that they wanted to scare me a bit so that I would bend to the system," he says. The charge was dropped after he submitted to a 90-day probation and a psychiatric evaluation. Leese was ordered to stay off school property, forcing him to miss all the senior activities planned for the end of the year—a banquet, a picnic, a dance. Then his principal, Superintendent Linda Hippert, relented. "I felt that Aaron needed to be punished, but my assumption after the investigation was that the punishment did not fit the crime," says Hippert. "I know Aaron very well, and what he was denied was above and beyond what he had done." With her blessing, Leese was allowed to graduate with his class.

12

Gun Control Is Needed to End School Shootings

Kathy Coffey

Kathy Coffey is a freelance writer and poet.

The shootings at Columbine High School compelled thousands of parents to take action and march in support of gun laws that will prevent further shootings. However, the gun lobby has prevented the passage of such legislation. Gun rights advocates should stop attacking the Million Mom March and other protests and recognize that grieving and fearful parents will not be thwarted in their efforts to protect their children.

She leaves, and I feel the same twinge of fear I have felt every morning since April 20, 1999. She goes gladly. She likes her school, Littleton High, located about 15 miles from Columbine. Her hair is an auburn mantle as she runs into the morning, a clatter of keys, books and backpack. In the 15-year-old world of my youngest daughter, the details are pressing, the larger picture distant.

Marching for gun control

But Columbine has affected my world, as I suspect it has for many parents. We do not take lightly the hurried goodbye, the last "I love you" tossed across the quiet morning. It even changes my usual Mother's Day pattern of lounging, planting flowers, enjoying the luxury of a dinner cooked by my four children. Instead, I drive with two daughters to Denver's civic center, crowded with 12,000 other moms, children and dads. We imagine our gathering repeated around the country, and cheer the figures announced from Washington, D.C.: 500,000 in the Million Mom March there.

Many gathered here in Denver are veterans of other demonstrations: the civil rights marches, the protests against the war in Vietnam and the School of the Americas in Georgia. Graying liberals, we joke about introducing our kids to the fine subversion of the 60's. But beneath the banter, we recognize that once again the underdogs are tackling the powerful status quo. For the umpteenth time we wonder what one can do against so many. Weakly, we boo the announcement that the National Rifle Association (N.R.A.) will spend $30 million to influence the fall elections.

N.R.A. members who encircle our protest hardly seem a threat. They accuse us of wanting slavery simply because we advocate gun locks. They shout freedom slogans, apparently unaware how un-nuanced and irrelevant they are to a discussion of background checks for gun buyers. The lettering on their T-shirts, "Tyranny Response Team," stretches taut over bulging beer-guts. Their attempt to drown out the music and dance of the demonstration with bullhorns sounds relentlessly dull. One tries not to think of gorillas thumping their chests. In true protest style, both sides wave the flag.

All the money in the world cannot contend with the rage of a mother torn from her child.

Yet we cannot dismiss them as thugs throwing testosterone tantrums. While these counter-protestors may not represent the cream of the crop, the gun lobby has a stranglehold on national and state legislatures. Because of their influence, no significant legislation has been passed in the year since Columbine to protect kids from gun violence.

And that makes their mothers mad. If catchy rhetoric is crucial to a cause, this one has some gems: "Woe to you who try to come between a mother and her child." "Take your gun and go to your room!" "The gun lobby is no match for a million moms." "We love our children more than they love their guns." "Our kids are more protected from an aspirin bottle than from a semi-automatic."

Why gun control is necessary

But all the slogans fade before the raw pain of Tom and Linda Mauser, whose son Daniel was killed at Columbine. "Honorary mom" for the day, Tom addresses the group gathered near the capitol where, 10 days after the slaughter, he spoke in public for the first time. His words now echo his words then: "I'm here because Daniel would expect me to be here."

Such a simple statement, yet it snags the breath in the throat. I pause in the act of applying sunscreen to my daughter's freckled shoulder. Suddenly the gesture is unbearably poignant. I think of all the moms who can no longer do this basic kindness for their children—12 a day murdered by guns. In Colorado, the litany of names has become a bracelet of memory: Cassie, Steven, Corey, Kelly, Matthew, Daniel, Rachel, Isaiah, John, Lauren, Dan, Kyle and their teacher Dave.

We know their stories and have memorized their faces. We saw the initial television footage, stunning and stark. The stretchers, the IV's, the sirens, the long procession of ambulances. In shock we endured the irony of funerals where the mourners, the pallbearers and the deceased were all under 18. Now we see the aftereffects: the wheelchairs, the surgeries, the rehabilitation that never quite restores the ambling lope of a 15-year-old boy, the slender grace of a 16-year-old girl.

Perhaps the N.R.A. has met its match. All the money in the world cannot contend with the rage of a mother torn from her child. They have tampered with some deep and primal instinct, and they cannot win. An initiative in Colorado for the November ballot aims to require background checks and close "the gun-show loophole." If the legislature cannot accomplish it, the people will. Every mom at that march has a vote—and as we are frequently reminded, a vote is a terrible thing to waste. We may be political neophytes, but we will master any system we must to protect the vulnerable child.

I know with stinging clarity that Lauren or Daniel could have been my daughter or son. My stomach churned when Dawn Anna, Lauren's mom, hugged her slain child's graduation cap and gown and called the valedictorian "a mother's dream." The gun that fired 11 bullets into Lauren was obtained as easily as "taking cereal off a grocery shelf." Despite a year of grieving, the stories remain heart-wrenching. I suspect we are ready to take the next step now, to make the transition from profound sorrow to vibrant action.

When people feel strongly about an issue, their language becomes direct and dramatic. "Enough," they say. "No more." The gun control measures proposed nationally and locally seem mild compared to those of other civilized nations. The statistics are clear, but the joined voice of the mothers roars even clearer. Listen intently and hear beneath them the tragic moans of students who thought a school library safe. Never again. Never another Columbine.

13

Gun Control Is Not the Answer to School Shootings

Joanne Eisen

Joanne Eisen is a research associate with the Independence Institute, a civil liberties think tank in Golden, Colorado.

Additional gun laws will not prevent school shootings. The best way to stop the occurrence of mass shootings is the passage of right-to-carry laws, which permit law-abiding adults to carry concealed weapons. These laws reduce violent crime because potential criminals are deterred by the possibility of being shot by one of their targets. In fact, shootings are more likely to occur at schools in vicinities where adults' access to handguns is restricted. Children should be taught that, under certain circumstances, violence might be needed for self-defense.

On April 20, 1999, after a year of planning—and signs of trouble ignored by parents, teachers and peers—Eric Harris and Dylan Klebold opened fire on fellow students at Columbine High School in Littleton, Colorado. When the shooting stopped, 12 classmates and a teacher were dead. So were Harris and Klebold from self-inflicted wounds. Fourteen others lay wounded.

The public—in America and elsewhere—was exposed to countless media pundits asking "Why Littleton?" Was it the parents' fault? Was it video games, or peer problems, or psychotropic prescription drugs?

Finding reasons for more gun laws

The response was predictable: Guns were used in committing the mayhem, and so somehow, it happened because of them. (Never mind they were intended for just a minor role in the calculated destruction.) Of course, all gun-owners—responsible, law-abiding or not—collectively share in the blame in the minds of the media and the politicians.

More "reasonable" gun laws needed? (Apparently, 20,000 are still not enough.) Too easy access to firearms? (The Brady Law was supposed to fix that.)

Reprinted, with permission, from "Ambush! Exploiting the Tragedy at Columbine," by Joanne Eisen, *Guns*, January 2000.

Within weeks, Congress was busy crafting more restrictive gun laws. Not laws that would address future Littletons—these were laws that firearm-prohibitionists had already prepared, well in advance, just lying in wait for the next outrageous tragedy so the public could be easily manipulated into accepting them.

These laws were designed to close all the "loopholes" which allow law-abiding American gun buyers to avoid government knowledge of their firearm acquisitions.

To those convinced that the only road to a safer society means getting rid of all the guns, consider this: What if filling your vague prescription for an ideal world fosters the very climate which created Littleton?

Concealed handgun laws can prevent shootings

A quarter of a century ago, in his 1971 book *Firearms Control*, which chronicled gun-control in Great Britain, Colin Greenwood made a timeless observation: ". . . one is forced to the rather startling conclusion that the use of firearms in crime was very much less when there were no controls of any sort and when anyone, convicted criminal or lunatic, could buy any type of firearm without restriction."

Greenwood is currently a researcher and forensic firearm examiner, with a background in both military and police work.

We can now explain statistically the basis for his non-politically-correct observations. According to University of Chicago researchers Drs. John Lott and William Landes, deaths and injuries from mass public shootings—like Littleton—fall dramatically after right-to-carry (liberalized) concealed handgun laws are enacted.

Would [Eric] Harris and [Dylan] Klebold have done what they did, knowing there was a good chance of being stopped dead in their tracks by an armed adult?

Analysis of data from 1977 to 1995 shows that the average death rate from mass shootings plummeted by up to 91 percent after such laws went into effect, and injuries dropped by over 80 percent! (Colorado was in the midst of considering just such a law when Littleton intervened.)

Lott explained: "People who engage in mass public shootings are deterred by the possibility that law-abiding citizens may be carrying guns. Such people may be deranged, but they still appear to care whether they will themselves be shot as they attempt to kill others."

Are you still convinced that guns are the cause of the recent rash of school shootings? If so, you must consider the fact that far fewer children today have legal access to or experience and training with guns. Maybe that's part of the problem. A July 1993 U.S. Department of Justice study found that "boys who own legal firearms . . . have much lower rates of delinquency and drug use [than those who obtained them illegally] and are even slightly less delinquent than nonowners of guns." It concluded "for legal gunowners, socialization appears to take place in the family: for illegal gunowners, it appears to take place on the street."

Stricter gun laws have served only to change the pattern of firearm access, fueling the black market. Forty years ago, kids could buy guns over the counter, and it was considered normal for them to carry and own guns for hunting and recreation. No Littleton-style shootings occurred in 1959, however.

Gun control makes schools less safe

What else is different, nowadays? "Gun-free" school zones are new—could that have played a role? Lott pointed out that these, indeed, make schools safer—not for our children, but for those bent on harming them. Lott and Landes noted that "the recent rash of public school shootings . . . raise[s] questions about the unintentional consequences of laws." In Footnote 10 of their latest research, released in April 1999, they elaborated:

"The five public school shootings took place after a 1995 federal law banned guns (including permitted concealed handguns) within a thousand feet of a school. The possibility exists that attempts to outlaw guns from schools, no matter how well meaning, may have produced perverse effects. Lott and Landes further pointed out that, during the 1977 to 1995 period of their study, 15 shootings occurred in schools where access to handguns by adults was highly restricted, and only one such shooting occurred where adults had ready access to handguns.

What? Allow responsible adults to carry firearms in our schools? How uncivilized! How unthinkable!

But to parents who now worry every day about the safety of their children in our public schools, what's the safest bet? Harris and Klebold were wildly successful, because they could be—nobody on the outside stopped them, not even the police!

In May 1999, Senator Charles Schumer ran true to form and called for more gun laws. But instead of increasing the safety of our children, his schemes will only serve to make it more difficult for law-abiding adults to obtain firearms for self-defense, and places our children in greater jeopardy, as the research of Lott and Landes shows so well.

Would Harris and Klebold still have done what they did, knowing there was a good chance of being stopped dead in their tracks by an armed adult, thereby robbing them of the publicity they sought, and the success they hoped for?

That's exactly what happened at a high school in Pearl, Mississippi, in 1997. Armed with a hunting rifle, 16-year-old Luke Woodham killed his ex-girlfriend and her close friend, then wounded seven other students. Earlier that morning, Woodham had stabbed his mother to death.

Frequently omitted from this account is one small detail: Assistant Principal Joel Myrick retrieved a handgun from his car, and interrupted Woodham's shooting spree, holding him at bay until police arrived. We won't find any simple, single answer, but teaching our children that violence is wrong under any circumstances—even when necessary to protect their own lives—conditions them to be victims and serves to devalue their lives in preference to the lives of killers.

The quick and easy knee-jerk response to "gun-violence" and incidents like Littleton—"ban all the guns"—may sound compassionate at first. But compassion like that is both misplaced and harmful, when truth and common sense are lacking.

Lott said it's "unlikely" these incidents will ever completely disappear. While incidents like Littleton will always be devastating to those concerned—the victims, the grieving families and friends—the "ban-the-guns" solution will, in the end, be far more disastrous and cost many more lives.

Emotion aside, one thing is certain: gun control won't stop the madness—it will only make it worse.

14

Access to Mental Health Treatment Can Prevent School Shootings

Saul Levine

Saul Levine is the director of the Institute for Behavioral Health at Children's Hospital and Health Center in San Diego and a professor and director of the Division of Child and Adolescent Psychiatry at the University of California, San Diego.

No single reason can be given to explain why school shootings occur, because every perpetrator has a unique personality and upbringing. However, psychiatric and psychological intervention can prevent troubled youth from committing violent acts. Despite its benefits, many children lack access to mental health treatment. Society needs to take steps to ensure that the necessary support systems are available for adolescents.

To the horror of all of us, we have once again been shocked by another tragedy in our schools. We are appalled, pained, enraged and confused. What is so wrong? Whom should we blame?

We have been besieged by media stories of students killing teachers, classmates and family members or themselves. What are we to conclude from the seemingly recent outbreak of lethal violence in schools across the country? This, in a time in America of relative prosperity and peace, quality of life and quiescence. Oregon, Arkansas, California, Washington, New York, and now Colorado—few states are unscathed, and everybody is affected.

A variety of explanations

What is going on, we wonder? Why is this happening? How do we deal with our pain, and perhaps most importantly, can we derive meanings, lessons, policies, from these truly terrifying events?

"Answers" to these questions come fast and furious. Social commen-

Reprinted, with permission, from "Who Is to Blame for Terror in Our Schools?" by Saul Levine, *San Diego Union-Tribune*, April 22, 1999.

tators claim that we are witnessing these acts because of moral deterioration and turpitude in our society. Gun-control advocates blame the maiming and murder on the incredible availability of handguns, rifles and semi-automatic weapons in this country. Seers say we are witnessing the natural results of liberalism, licentiousness and moral laxity in our nation.

Some say that we are a country which extols and glorifies violent solutions to interpersonal conflicts. They argue that a macho or manly reputation in America means force, domination, and perpetuation of egregious harm. Others blame movies, television, the Internet, the evening news, newspaper headlines and other media for our preoccupation with violence.

Liberal critics say that we have dismantled and removed social supports for children and families in communities and schools. Mental Health professionals decry the lack of resources and opportunities to work with these children and their families. Still others argue that these children are "bad seeds" and should be incarcerated in special detention facilities. These myriad perspectives, offered in an effort to elucidate and clarify the morass of complexity, leave us with no clear answers, and paradoxically, serve to confuse and perplex us further. We humans so need simplistic answers to life's inherent conundrums. We abhor ambiguity and confusion—they create anxiety and insecurity. We crave coherence and meaningfulness—they comfort and reassure us. We all look for easy answers to the extraordinary complexities of life. The problem with simplistic punditry, however, is that it often avoids facts: it is based on educated conjecture, but, in a rush to judgment, highly complicated situations often are reduced to sound bites, and simplistic solutions.

No specific profile

Let us examine exactly what it is that we *do* know:

• These events, as shocking as they are, do not represent a new phenomenon. There are thousands of historical and clinical instances, and records, of children and adolescents perpetrating heinous acts of brutality on kith and kin, both in times of peace and in time of social upheaval.

• The school killings are not restricted to the inner city. In case you didn't notice, most of the recent mayhem has occurred in middle America—middle class, Caucasian, intact families, in religious, closely-knit communities. In the '80s, we were preoccupied with gang-inspired terror and violence in inner-city communities and schools. Now, we see that no community is completely immune to the dark side of our souls.

• The young perpetrators do not represent one type of personality, one diagnosis or identical problems. They vary widely in their backgrounds, levels of social supports, histories of difficulties, family relationships and nature of communities. Some are disturbed, some have been abused, and some seem to be like "the kid next door". We do know that the majority are male, tend to have problems with anger, and are usually not in the mainstream of popularity, sports, or scholastic excellence. But, in truth, tomorrow we might hear of a brilliant, popular girl who committed a brutal act. Each case has to be carefully examined on a specific basis, to see what commonalties predispose to these horrific behaviors, and how we can try to prevent these acts in the future. One size does not fit all. Just as different children explode for different reasons, the punishment and/or treatment will vary with age, personality, and circumstances.

• Similarly, the families differ widely from each other. Some are dysfunctional, rife with alcohol, abuse and conflict. Others have been through divorce(s) and schisms. Still others seem to be, at least to the outside observer, committed, cohesive and caring.

• There are just too many guns available and accessible to our youth (one is too many, in my opinion). The firing of a lethal weapon of destruction at another human being leads to irrevocable harm. Yes, one can maim and kill with rope, chain, bats or knives, etc., but these instruments at least have other uses (other than killing), one can more easily avoid death and recover from wounds, and not as many individuals can simultaneously fall victims to a youngster with murderous intent. That we are the only country in the world which allows (or even encourages) our youth to utilize lethal devices of death should be a national shame and disgrace, a betrayal of what our Founding Fathers ever envisioned.

Mental health treatment can help

• Psychological and psychiatric intervention is not an absolute protection, but we know of so many cases and circumstances in which troubled children and adolescents have been helped and have had their antisocial urges eradicated. We also know of cases in which youngsters have been actively and successfully dissuaded from committing dangerous acts (to themselves or others) and cases in which authorities have been advised about the possibility of violence, and preventive measures have been successfully instituted. This is not to say that mental health treatment is a universal panacea; some of the murderous children had in fact seen a therapist. But, in most instances, the acts could have been circumvented with early medical and psychological treatment for the children and families.

Better social supports, preventive techniques, earlier intervention and communal values would greatly diminish the implosive torment of disturbed young people.

• We have made it much more difficult for troubled children to get appropriate treatment. Managed care and fiscal restraints have turned already inaccessible health care into an impossible and intolerable system for some disturbed children. Similarly, as social supports for families and communities are increasingly dismantled, those who are particularly vulnerable are put in even more jeopardy and at risk.

• It does, in fact, take a village. This perspective is not a paean to Hillary Clinton's book, as much as it is to the sentiment of the Swahili saying on which it is based ("It takes a village to raise a child"). In the same vein, we are, or should be, our brother's keeper. Perhaps if we believed and taught our children that we are part of a larger human community, beyond ourselves, we would take heed of expressed worries and warnings of classmates, neighbors or others who are clearly troubled.

• We are *not* witnessing the decline and fall of the American civilization. Notwithstanding "The Jerry Springer Show," we are not descending into the abyss of Sodom and Gomorrah. The vast majority of our youth find lethal weapons and violence as abhorrent as do civilized adults. This country's children and adolescents are full of promise, idealism and commitment. They are full of energy and dedication, just "waiting" to be captivated by lofty ideals and values.

While there are no guarantees in life, better social supports, preventive techniques, earlier intervention and communal values would greatly diminish the implosive torment of disturbed young people and their explosive aftermath.

Organizations to Contact

The editors have compiled the following list of organizations concerned with the issues debated in this book. The descriptions are derived from materials provided by the organizations. All have publications or information available for interested readers. The list was compiled on the date of publication of the present volume; the information provided here may change. Be aware that many organizations take several weeks or longer to respond to inquiries, so allow as much time as possible.

American Civil Liberties Union (ACLU)
132 W. 43rd St., New York, NY 10036
(212) 944-9800 • fax: (212) 869-9065
e-mail: aclu@aclu.org • website: www.aclu.org

The ACLU champions the rights set forth in the Declaration of Independence and the U.S. Constitution. The ACLU interprets the Second Amendment as a guarantee for states to form militias, not as a guarantee of the individual right to own and bear firearms. Consequently, the organization believes that gun control is constitutional and, since guns are dangerous, it is necessary. It opposes many of the steps taken by schools to prevent shootings, including zero-tolerance policies, security cameras, and restrictions on freedom of expression, arguing that such policies violate students' rights. The ACLU publishes the semiannual *Civil Liberties* in addition to policy statements and reports.

Brady Campaign to Prevent Gun Violence
1225 Eye St. NW, Suite 1100, Washington, DC 20005
(202) 898-0792 • fax: (202) 371-9615
website: www.bradycampaign.org

Handgun Control is an organization that campaigns for regulations on the manufacture, sale, and civilian possession of handguns and automatic weapons. Its publications include the issue briefs "Kids & Guns" and "Preventing Crime & Prosecuting Criminals," along with studies on the impact on crime of the Brady law and other gun control measures.

Center for the Prevention of School Violence
313 Chapanoke Rd., Suite 140, Raleigh, NC 27603
(800) 299-6054 • fax: (919) 773-2904
website: www.ncsu.edu/cpsv/

The center is a primary resource in the problem of school violence. Its mission is to ensure that children can attend safe and secure schools. The center and its website provide information, research, and program assistance for schools in North Carolina and throughout the United States. The center publishes newsletters and research bulletins.

Coalition to Stop Gun Violence (CSGV)/Educational Fund to Stop Gun Violence
1000 16th St. NW, Suite 603, Washington, DC 20002
(202) 530-0340 • fax: (202) 530-0331
e-mail: webmaster@csgv.org • website: www.csgv.org

The CSGV lobbies at the local, state, and federal levels to ban the sale of handguns to individuals and to institute licensing and registration of all firearms. It also litigates cases against firearms makers. Its publications include various informational sheets on gun violence and the *Annual Citizens' Conference to Stop Gun Violence Briefing Book*, a compendium of gun control fact sheets, arguments, and resources. Its sister organization, the Educational Fund to Stop Gun Violence, is dedicated to stopping gun violence by fostering effective community and national action. The Educational Fund provides organizations and individuals with the tools to reduce gun violence effectively through educational outreach to researchers, educators, journalists, attorneys, legislators and the general public. The fund publishes the bimonthly newsletter *Stop Gun Violence*. The website offers research on school violence.

ERIC Clearinghouse on Educational Management: School Safety and Violence Prevention
University of Oregon, 1787 Agate St., Eugene, OR 97403-5207
(800) 438-8841• fax: (541) 346-2334
e-mail: eric@eric.uoregon.edu
website: eric.uoregon.edu/trends_issues/safety/

The Educational Resources Information Center (ERIC) is a nationwide educational information system. The staff of the Clearinghouse on Educational Management acquires and organizes information on educational management. In addition, the clearinghouse produces a variety of books, monographs, and papers. Among its publications are the monograph *Safe School Design* and digests on school safety.

National Rifle Association of America (NRA)
11250 Waples Mill Rd., Fairfax, VA 22030
(703) 267-1000 • fax: (703) 267-3989
website: www.nra.org

With nearly 3 million members, the NRA is America's largest organization of gun owners. It is also the primary lobbying group for those who oppose gun control laws. The NRA believes that such laws violate the U.S. Constitution and do nothing to reduce crime. In addition to its monthly magazines *America's 1st Freedom, American Rifleman, American Hunter, InSights,* and *Shooting Sports USA*, the NRA publishes numerous books, bibliographies, reports, and fact sheets on school safety and gun control. The NRA asserts that most schools are safe and additional gun legislation laws will not prevent school shootings from occurring.

National School Boards Association (NSBA)
1680 Duke St., Alexandria, VA 22314
(703) 838-6722 • fax: (703) 683-7590
e-mail: info@nsba.org • website: www.nsba.org

The association develops projects that help school boards strengthen and reform public schools. It supports zero-tolerance policies to help reduce school violence. The NSBA publishes the *American School Board Journal* and the newsletter *Updating School Board Policies*.

National School Safety Center (NSSC)
141 Duesenberg Dr., Suite 11, Westlake Village, CA 91362
(805) 373-9977 • fax: (805) 373-9277
e-mail: info@nssc1.org • website: www.nssc1.org

Part of Pepperdine University, the center is a research organization that studies school crime and violence and provides technical assistance to local school systems. Its website provides statistics and resources on school violence. NSSC believes that teacher training is an effective way of reducing juvenile crime. Its publications include the book *School Safety Check Book*, the *School Safety Update* newsletter, published nine times a year, and the resource papers "Safe Schools Overview" and "Weapons in Schools."

Office of Juvenile Justice and Delinquency Prevention (OJJDP)
U.S. Department of Justice
Office of Justice Programs
PO Box 6000, Rockville, MD 20850
(800) 732-3277
e-mail: askJJ@ojp.usdoj.gov • website: ojjdp.ncjrs.org/gun/index.html

OJJDP provides national leadership and resources to prevent and respond to juvenile delinquency. It supports community efforts to develop effective programs and improve the juvenile justice system. Publications available at its website include "School House Hype: School Shootings and the Real Risks Kids Face in America" and "Kids and Guns: From Playground to Battlegrounds."

Violence Policy Center
1140 19th St. NW, Suite 600, Washington, DC 20036
(202) 822-8200 • fax: (202) 822-8205
website: www.vpc.org

The center is an educational foundation that conducts research on firearms violence. It works to educate the public concerning the dangers of guns and supports gun-control measures. The center's publications include *Start 'Em Young: Recruitment of Kids to the Gun Culture* and *Joe Camel with Feathers: How the NRA with Gun and Tobacco Industry Dollars Uses its Eddie Eagle Program to Market Guns to Kids.*

Youth Crime Watch of America (YCWA)
9300 S. Dadeland Blvd., Suite 100, Miami, FL 33156
(305) 670-2409 • fax: (305) 670-3805
e-mail: ycwa@ycwa.org • website: www.ycwa.org

YCWA is a nonprofit, student-led organization that promotes crime and drug prevention programs in communities and schools throughout the United States. Member-students at the elementary and secondary level help raise others' awareness concerning alcohol and drug abuse, crime, gangs, guns, and the importance of staying in school. Strategies include organizing student assemblies and patrols, conducting workshops, and challenging students to become personally involved in preventing crime and violence. YCWA publishes the quarterly newsletter *National Newswatch* and the *Community Based Youth Crime Watch Program Handbook.*

Bibliography

Books

Elliot Aronson	*Nobody Left to Hate: Teaching Compassion After Columbine.* New York: Worth Publishers, 2000.
Denise M. Bonilla, ed.	*School Violence.* New York: H.W. Wilson, 2000.
Carl Bosch	*Schools Under Siege: Guns, Gangs, and Hidden Dangers.* Springfield, NJ: Enslow Publishers, 1997.
Vic Cox	*Guns, Violence, and Teens.* Springfield, NJ: Enslow, 1997.
Raymond B. Flannery Jr.	*Preventing Youth Violence: A Guide for Parents, Teachers, and Counselors.* New York: Continuum, 1999.
Jib Fowles	*The Case for Television Violence.* Thousand Oaks, CA: Sage Publications, 1999.
SuEllen Fried and Paula Fried	*Bullies & Victims: Helping Your Children Through the Schoolyard Battlefield.* New York: M. Evans and Company, 1996.
Dave Grossman and Gloria DeGaetano	*Stop Teaching Our Kids to Kill: A Call to Action Against TV, Movie, and Video Game Violence.* New York: Crown, 1999.
Kathleen M. Heide	*Young Killers: The Challenge of Juvenile Homicide.* Thousand Oaks, CA: Sage Publications, 1999.
William G. Hinkle and Stuart Henry, eds.	*School Violence.* Thousand Oaks, CA: Sage Publications, 2000.
Allan M. Hoffman, ed.	*Schools, Violence, and Society.* Westport, CT: Praeger, 1996.
Bob Larson	*Extreme Evil: Kids Killing Kids.* Nashville: T. Nelson Publishers, 1999.
Madeline Levine	*Viewing Violence: How Media Violence Affects Your Child and Adolescent's Development.* New York: Doubleday, 1996.
Joy D. Osofsky, ed.	*Children in a Violent Society.* New York: Guilford Press, 1997.
Public Agenda	*Violent Kids: Can We Change the Trend?* Dubuque, IA: Kendall/Hunt, 2000.
Ted Schwarz	*Kids and Guns: The History, the Present, the Dangers, and the Remedies.* New York: Franklin Watts, 1999.
Wendy Murray Zoba	*Day of Reckoning: Columbine and the Search for America's Soul.* Grand Rapids, MI: Brazos Press, 2000.

Periodicals

Tom Allen	"Keep Guns Out of School," *Virginia Journal of Education,* October 1998. Available from Virginia Education Association, 116 S. Third St., Richmond, VA 23219.

Dale Anema	"A Father at Columbine High," *American Enterprise*, September 1999. Available from 1150 17th St. NW, Washington, DC 20036.
Christopher Caldwell	"Levittown to Littleton," *National Review*, May 31, 1999.
Dana Charry and Ellen Charry	"The Crisis of Violence," *Christian Century*, July 15, 1998.
Deedee Corradini	"Making Schools Safe for Kids," *USA Today*, May 1999.
Thomas De Zengotita	"The Gunfire Dialogues," *Harper's Magazine*, July 1999.
David Grossman	"Trained to Kill," *Christianity Today*, August 10, 1998.
Albert R. Hunt	"Teen Violence Spawned by Guns and Cultural Rot," *Wall Street Journal*, June 11, 1998.
Gary Kleck	"School Lesson: Armed Self-Defense Works," *Wall Street Journal*, March 27, 2001.
Dave Kopel	"Children as the '90s Wedge Issue," *Gun News Digest*, Winter 1998/1999. Available from 12500 NE Tenth Pl., Bellevue, WA 98005.
Anne C. Lewis	"Listen to the Children," *Phi Delta Kappan*, June 1999.
John R. Lott Jr.	"Availability of Guns Is Not the Cause of Youth Violence," *Insight on the News*, July 24, 2000. Available from 3600 New York Ave. NE, Washington, DC 20002.
Nancy B. Miner	"Warning Signals from Disturbed Youth," *USA Today*, September 2000.
Peggy Noonan	"The Culture of Death," *Wall Street Journal*, April 22, 1999.
Ann Powers	"The Stresses of Youth, The Strains of Its Music," *New York Times*, April 25, 1999.
Judith A. Reisman	"Cultivating Killers," *New American*, June 7, 1999. Available from 770 Westhill Blvd., Appleton, WI 54914.
Vincent Schiraldi	"Making Sense of Juvenile Homicides in America," *America*, July 17, 1999.
Darrell Scott	"Columbine Tragedy Shows Nation Must Return to a Trust in God," *Insight on the News*, May 1, 2000.
Tom Teepen	"Gunning for Pop Culture," *Liberal Opinion Week*, May 17, 1999. Available from PO Box 880, Vinton, IA 52349-0880.

Index

(SERV), 55
Sanders, Dave, 39
Sawyer, Diane, 30
Schiraldi, Vincent, 7–8
schools
  culture of, 10–12
  expulsion from, 60–61
  prevention of shootings in
    and counselors, 52
    and educators, 60
      training of, 54, 57
        curricula for, 53, 54
    programs, 52, 54, 55
  suspension from, 60–61
  uniforms in, 52
  zero-tolerance policies of, 53
  see also bullying; educators; guns;
    security; violence
Schumer, Charles, 67
security
  at Columbine High School, 8
  cost of, 59
  described, 8, 52–53, 59, 60
  environment created by
    can be nurturing, 61
    helplessness, 56, 60
    impedes learning, 60
    is that of a police state, 31
    is unconstitutional, 59
    may increase violence, 60–61
  ignores real problems, 27
Sega Dreamcast, 16–17
Shapiro, Bruce, 31–32
shooter games. *See* video games
shooters
  alienation of, 13, 14
  bullying of, 8, 27
  presented as victims by media, 14
  profile of, 41, 70
60 Minutes (TV program), 17
Spector, Warren, 26
Stango, Alice, 58
Stango, Bobby, 58
Sterngold, James, 8
Stop Teaching Our Kids to Kill (Grossman
  and DeGaetano), 22
suicide, 38

technology, numbing effect of, 20–21
teenagers
  brain of, and immaturity, 48
  characteristics of, 28
  decrease in violence by, 8
  lack access to mental health services,
    69, 71
  must learn to be more tolerant, 8
  suicide by, 38

violence as part of lives of, 12
television. *See* media
Time (magazine), 11
Trench Coat Mafia, 27–28
20/20 (TV program), 30

Unreal (video game), 26
U.S. News & World Report (magazine), 42

video games
  are form of military training, 22
  in Asia, 31
  described, 18–19
  effects of, 24
    are same as television, 21
  importance of speed in, 18
  popularity of, 17, 28
  racism in, 22–23
  rating of, 23
  shooter games, 19–20, 26
  violence of
    desensitizes gamers, 16, 20
    does not transfer to reality, 25
violence
  access to guns decreases, 36, 67
  in American culture, 23, 70
  belief that it is an African American
    problem, 40–42
  causes of, are unknown, 32, 35
  decrease in, 27
  exposure to, 21, 30
  geographic distribution of, 70
  and gun control laws, 34, 37–38, 53,
    65
  is part of adolescence, 12
  physiological explanation of, 47,
    48–49
  in language, 56–58
  in literature, 11
  in schools
    frequency of, 7–8
    has decreased, 27
    is exaggerated, 7, 28
    religion will decrease, 35
    security measures may increase,
      60–61
  by U.S. military is sanctioned, 29
  see also bullying; media; video games

Wall Street Journal (newspaper), 7
Weinberger, Daniel R., 47
Williams, Charles Andrew, 15, 34
Wise, Tim, 40
Woodham, Luke, 67

Zombie, Rob, 12
Zuckor, Brian, 15